Reading Matters 1

Reading Matters 1

An Interactive Approach to Reading

Mary Lee Wholey

Continuing Education Language Institute
Concordia University

HOUGHTON MIFFLIN COMPANY   Boston   New York

Director of ESL Programs: Susan Maguire
Senior Associate Editor: Kathleen Sands Boehmer
Editorial Assistant: Manuel Muñoz
Senior Project Editor: Kathryn Dinovo
Senior Cover Design Coordinator: Deborah Azerrad Savona
Senior Manufacturing Coordinator: Priscilla Bailey
Marketing Manager: Jay Hu
Marketing Associate: Claudia Martinez

Cover design and image: Harold Burch, Harold Burch Design, New York City

Text and graph credits p. 98: "A measure of happiness," (2/9/99), copyright 1999, USA Today. Reprinted with permission. p. 165: "Mobile phone growth markets," (2/19/99), copyright 1999, USA Today. Reprinted with permission. p. 188: "Household technology penetration," (11/20/97), copyright 1997, USA Today. Reprinted with permission. p. 196: from *The Overworked American,* by Juliet B. Schor. Copyright © 1991 by BasicBooks, a division of HarperCollins Publishers, Inc. Reprinted by permission of Basic Books, a member of Perseus Books, L.L.C. p. 227: Newsweek, "Traveling on the American Plan," © 1998 Newsweek, Inc. All rights reserved. Reprinted by permission.

Photo Credits p. 1: Gary A. Connor/Photo Edit; p. 2: Robert Brenner/Photo Edit; p. 6: Tom Petty/Photo Edit; p. 39: Michael Newman/Photo Edit; p. 40:Ted Spagna/Photo Researchers, Inc.; p.49: Spencer Grant/Photo Edit; p. 53: Dion Ogust/The Image Works; p. 73: Richard Shock/Tony Stone Images; p. 74: R. Lord/The Image Works; p. 85: Ariel Skelley/The Stock Market; p. 89: AP/Wide World Photos; p. 101: Hal Charms/Photo Edit; p. 111: F. Pedrick/The Image Works; p. 112: Bob Daemmrich/Stock Boston; p. 123: Mike Chew/The Stock Market; p. 123: Bill Bachman/ Photo Researchers, Inc.; p. 129: Bill Truslow/Tony Stone Images; p. 129: Paul Souders/Tony Stone Images; p. 140: Topham/The Image Works; p. 151: David Nunuk/Science Photo Library/Photo Researchers, Inc.; p. 152: Liaison Agency/Photo copyright University of Pennsylvania; p. 155: Hank Morgan/Photo Researchers, Inc.; p. 163: Hans Hendrikse; p. 166: Paul Harris/Tony Stone Images; p. 166: David Rosenberg/Tony Stone Images; p. 181: Robert Levine/The Stock Market; p. 193: Peter Saloutos/The Stock Market; 194: James Harrington/Tony Stone Images; p. 205: Ariel Skelley/The Stock Market; p. 208: Tony Freeman/Photo Edit; p. 212: Gamma /Liaison Agency; p. 220: Kunio Owaki/The Stock Market; p. E–3: Colin Jones/Panos Pictures, London; p. E–5: Courtesy of The Spiritual Life Institute, Nada Hermitage, Crestone, CO

Post-it® Notes is a registered trademark of 3M Company.

www.hmco.com/college

Printed in the U.S.A.

Library of Congress Catalog Card Number: 99-71902

ISBN: 0-395-90426-9

3 4 5 6 7 8 9 – CRS – 04 03 02 01

Contents

v

Introduction

The *Reading Matters* series is a four-level reading program comprising texts at the high-beginning/low-intermediate, intermediate, high-intermediate, and advanced levels. This series combines stimulating readings with well-designed tasks that develop both fluency and accuracy at each level.

Extensive Reading

To develop fluency in reading, students need a significant amount of exposure to text, that is, extensive reading. Extensive reading provides the opportunity to develop automatic text-processing skills. *Reading Matters* offers reading selections of sufficient length so that readers get the chance to increase the amount of time spent in silent reading. Variety in text styles is an important component of extensive reading. The series features a variety of styles and genres so that readers develop an awareness of not only the scope of reading but also the various purposes for which texts are written. Authentic texts or adapted authentic texts are used at appropriate levels.

Intensive Reading

Reading Matters features activities that help students to develop fluency and accuracy in reading by activating two complementary text-processing methods: top-down and bottom-up.

TOP-DOWN

Top-down processes are those that the reader applies to understand reading globally. Readers use their background knowledge of the topic and make predictions about what they expect to find out from reading. Readers confirm their predictions and begin to build a mental framework of the information in the reading selection. Awareness of rhetorical patterns, such as chronological ordering, cause and effect, and other discourse features, aids in the comprehension of information from reading. In addition, the activities in *Reading*

Matters help to develop an awareness of a range of reading strategies, such as skimming, scanning, or previewing, that readers have at their disposal. The ability to apply these strategies appropriately is an important component of reading competency.

BOTTOM-UP

Knowledge of grammar and vocabulary has an effect on reading ability. Although readers can predict content from their knowledge of text structure or their background knowledge, a certain level of vocabulary recognition is required for processing text. *Reading Matters* introduces and develops vocabulary-building skills through such activities as guessing from context, recognizing meaning, grouping words, and identifying the use of special terms. In addition to a solid vocabulary, fluent readers have a good knowledge of syntactic structure. Actively examining the important grammatical features of a text provides a meaningful context for this kind of learning. To build reading competency, both the amount of exposure to reading and the identification of and practice in the use of learning strategies for both vocabulary and grammar are tremendously important. *Reading Matters* provides direction to readers through activities in the "Vocabulary Building," "Expanding Your Language," and "Read On" sections.

Skills Integration and Interaction

Reading is an active process. Interaction between and among students helps to facilitate this process. In exchanging ideas about the information in a text, readers confirm what they have understood. This confirmation process helps them to develop accuracy in reading. It also provides a motivation for reading, as well as a clear purpose in reading. Interaction with other students can be best accomplished when speaking tasks are an integral part of a reading activity or the activity leads to the undertaking of writing tasks.

The interrelationship of skills integration and interaction requires a holistic approach to task design. The activities in *Reading Matters* are sequenced, and the recycling of tasks in various combinations allows the progressive development of reading competency in ways that are fresh and effective. The tasks are structured so that the learner builds skills and strategies progressively but in ways that offer challenge as well as variety. In *Reading Matters,* the reader uses and reuses the language of the selection both implicitly to bolster an answer and explicitly in retelling the reading. Paired reading selections provide complementary or contrasting information on a topic. The readers orally explain the information from the reading they chose to readers who chose a different selection. Then, together, they apply that information to carry out a new activity.

Text Organization

Reading Matters 1 contains six thematic units, with three chapters in each unit. Each chapter features one or two reading selections. The unit themes develop topics of high interest to both academically oriented and general audiences. Most important, the selections are long enough for students to progressively gain fluency in reading. Through the chapter readings, students are able to build a rich semantic network without sacrificing variety, so that their interest in the topic is not exhausted. Within each unit, reading selections are structured so that the information from one selection can be compared with another.

You can choose among the chapters of a unit to suit the needs of various program types and teaching approaches. Complexity in both text style and length and difficulty in task type are structured to build gradually from chapter to chapter and unit to unit. Some overlap in level of language and task is built into each of the texts in the *Reading Matters* series so that you can accommodate the various reading levels of students within a class.

UNIT ORGANIZATION

Each unit in *Reading Matters 1* features the following components:

- "Introducing the Topics." This introductory section identifies the theme. It features the unit opener photo and quote, which are designed to stimulate the readers' curiosity, prior experience with the theme, or its personal relevance. The tasks are interactive and draw on a variety of media: text, visual, and graphic.

- The three chapters in each unit present various topics loosely related to the theme.

CHAPTER ORGANIZATION

For each of the reading selections, the following tasks are presented:

- "Chapter Openers" include prereading reflection and discussion questions, graphs, questionnaires, surveys, or illustrations. The purpose of this section is to stimulate discussion of key ideas and concepts presented in the reading and to introduce key vocabulary. Encourage students to explain their ideas as completely as possible. Teach students strategies for maximizing their interaction, such as taking turns, eliciting responses from all group members, and naming a group leader and reporter. Whenever possible, re-form groups to give students a chance to talk more until they feel comfortable with the topic. Elicit key ideas and language from the students.

- "Exploring and Understanding Reading" contains content questions of varying levels of complexity. These questions guide students in the development of their reading strategies for improving general comprehension, for developing an awareness of text structure, and for evaluating the content of a text in detail. Emphasize the purpose of the activity and how it is tied to the development of a particular strategy. Help students to build up their tolerance for uncertainty. Point out that the purpose of comparing and checking their answers with the information in the reading is to verify and to become familiar with the information in the reading. Act as a resource to help students find the accurate information. An answer key is provided to be used when needed.

- "Paired Readings: Recapping, Retelling, and Reacting to the Reading" present interactive activities that involve oral presentation of information from the readings, oral exchanges of information, and discussion that involves critical evaluation of ideas, including comparison/contrast and debate. Emphasize the importance of explaining the information in as natural and conversational a style as possible. To help students develop their skill at extracting important information from a text, point out the purpose of and methodology for taking notes, highlighting, and underlining key information. Emphasize the importance of practicing at home for in-class presentations.

- "Vocabulary Building" comprises tasks that introduce vocabulary-building strategies for understanding the interrelationship of grammatical structure and meaning, using context cues, and developing other aids to the fluent processing of reading selections.

- "Expanding Your Language" presents activities that offer students other opportunities to use the material and strategies. Encourage students to use these activities to further their own comprehension of the readings. Through these activities, students can improve their speaking and writing fluency.

- "Read On: Taking It Further" presents activities that offer students opportunities for personal reading and related activities, including suggestions for further reading and reading and writing journal entries, vocabulary logs, and word play. Although most of this work is done outside of class, time can be found in the class schedule to report on some of the activities. This gives students a purpose for the work and practice in developing their reading skills and strategies.

Acknowledgments

I am grateful to Susan Maguire, who first suggested the idea for the series. A special thanks goes to Kathy Sands Boehmer, who has been an invaluable help throughout the lengthy process of bringing this manuscript into its present form. Thanks also to Kevin Evans and the rest of the production and editorial staff at Houghton Mifflin.

My gratitude to the people who read the manuscript and offered useful suggestions and critical comments: Richard Appelbaum, Broward Community College, Fort Lauderdale, FL; Jennifer Castello, Canada College, Redwood City, CA; Mary DiStephano Diaz, Broward Community College, Fort Lauderdale, FL; Stephen Drinane, Rockland Community College, Suffurn, NY; Sally Gearheart, Santa Rosa Junior College, Santa Rosa, CA; Barbara Hockman, City College of San Francisco, San Francisco, CA; and Sharilyn Wood, North Harris College, Houston, TX.

I would like to acknowledge the support and inspiring work of colleagues and students at the Continuing Education Language Institute (CELI) of Concordia University in Montreal. A special thanks goes to Adrianne Sklar for her advice and suggestions after reading drafts of the material. The continuing support of Lili Ullmann, Phyllis Vogel, and Nadia Henein has been invaluable to me. Thanks to Tanya Ullmann, who helped in the preparation of the answer key.

Finally, thanks to my family—Jerry, Jonah, and Yael—who haven't given up on me, even though they've heard "Can't right now, got to finish this work" for years on end.

Mary Lee Wholey

Reading Matters 1: Overview

UNIT	SKILLS	ACTIVITIES	VOCABULARY	EXPANSION
UNIT 1 Communication: Talking to Each Other	• previewing titles (1) • asking questions before reading (2) • using illustrations to retell information (2) • predicting (3)	• getting information from illustrations (1) • matching ideas and details (1) • problem solving (1) • recapping, retelling, and comparing stories (2) • matching pictures and captions (3) • matching questions and answers (3)	• using context to guess meaning (1) • categorizing (1) • going from general to specific information (2) • prepositions (3)	• answering a questionnaire (1, 2) • personal writing (1, 2) • role playing (3) • topic writing (3)
UNIT 2 The Mysteries of Sleep	• previewing a reading (4, 6) • Note taking; identifying key words (5) • reading an advice column (5) • identifying a speaker (6)	• answering a questionnaire (4) • problem solving (4) • recapping, reacting to, and retelling a story (5) • applying the information: solving a problem (5) • getting information from illustrations (6) • evaluating information (6)	• vocabulary in context: nouns and verbs (4, 6) • jigsaw sentences (4, 5) • categorizing (5) • using context to guess meaning (6)	• asking questions and giving answers (4) • role playing (5) • 2-minute taped talk (5) • discussion questions (6) • topic writing (6)
UNIT 3 Relationships	• predicting information (7) • marking questions in the margin (7) • understanding the main ideas (8) • previewing (9)	• identifying a speaker (7) • categorizing information (7) • getting information from an illustration (8) • completing a chart (8) • looking for similarities and differences between two stories (8) • agreeing and disagreeing (9) • note taking (9)	• vocabulary in context (7) • verb forms (7) • matching meanings (8) • vocabulary in context: nouns and adjectives (9) • prepositions (9)	• role playing an interview (7) • writing information from an interview (7) • role playing an argument (8) • personal writing (8, 9) • talking about benefits and problems (9)

Reading Matters 1: Overview *(continued)*

UNIT	SKILLS	ACTIVITIES	VOCABULARY	EXPANSION
UNIT 4 The Challenge of Sports Today	▪ reading in groups of words (10) ▪ predicting informa- tion (10) ▪ identifying the main ideas of para- graphs (10) ▪ note taking: listing the facts (11) ▪ comparing informa- tion from two readings (11) ▪ identifying support- ing points and details (12)	▪ answering informa- tion questions (10) ▪ note taking (10) ▪ evaluating the infor- mation: making a decision (10) ▪ recapping, reacting to, and retelling a story (11) ▪ getting facts from a chart (12) ▪ using information to complete a chart (12)	▪ antonyms (10) ▪ word form: noun endings (10) ▪ guessing meaning from context (10) ▪ jigsaw sentences (11) ▪ vocabulary in context: adjectives (11) ▪ vocabulary in context: past and present (12)	▪ making an oral presentation (10) ▪ preparing a ques- tionnaire (11) ▪ 2-minute taped talk (11) ▪ role playing (12) ▪ topic writing (12)
UNIT 5 Technology for Today's World	▪ previewing (13) ▪ finding advantages and disadvantages (13) ▪ locating and high- lighting important information (14) ▪ predicting informa- tion (15) ▪ understanding examples (15)	▪ getting information from illustrations (13) ▪ agreeing and dis- agreeing (13) ▪ making an argument (13) ▪ making a chart to list facts (14) ▪ recapping, reacting to, and retelling a story (14) ▪ applying informa- tion: problem solving (15)	▪ vocabulary in con- text (13) ▪ linking with "instead of" and "but" (13) ▪ recognizing defini- tions for technical terms (14) ▪ vocabulary in context: verbs (14)	▪ asking information questions (13) ▪ 2-minute taped talk (14) ▪ topic writing (14) ▪ making a question- naire (14, 15)
UNIT 6 Leisure	▪ using question words to find information (16) ▪ understanding examples (16) ▪ recognizing advan- tages and disad- vantages (17) ▪ finding main ideas (18) ▪ using highlighting to make a list (18)	▪ giving your opinion (16) ▪ asking questions (16) ▪ listing advantages and disadvantages (17) ▪ identifying a speaker (18) ▪ evaluating infor- mation: giving your opinion (18)	▪ vocabulary in con- text: nouns and verbs (16) ▪ antonyms (16) ▪ matching meanings (16) ▪ categorizing (17)	▪ 2-minute taped talk (16) ▪ interviewing (16) ▪ reviewing a movie (17) ▪ reaction writing (17) ▪ writing advantages and disadvan- tages (18)

Communication: Talking to Each Other

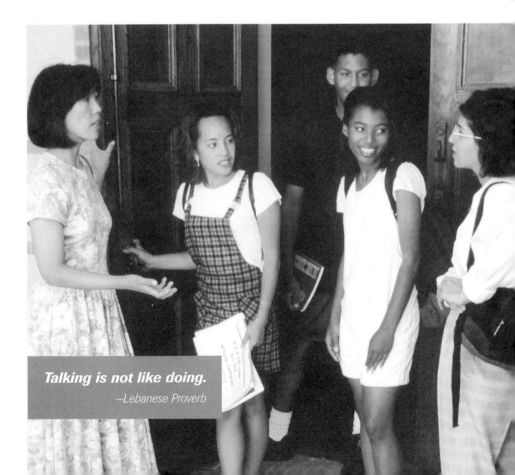

Talking is not like doing.
—Lebanese Proverb

Introducing the Topics

We communicate in many ways. In this unit, we will find out about some common forms of communication. Chapter 1 is about nonverbal communication, or body language. In Chapter 2, we will find out about two interesting cases of multilingual communication. Chapter 3 presents the story of Post-it® Notes, those handy pads of paper that are used for leaving messages everywhere.

Points of Interest

What do you think these people are trying to say?

CHAPTER 1

Reading Body Language

Chapter Openers

DISCUSSION QUESTIONS: COMMUNICATING WITHOUT WORDS

Think about these questions. Share your ideas with a partner or with a small group.

1. What is body language?

2. How do we learn to use and understand it?

3. Why is it important to understand body language?

4. Is it possible to read body language the wrong way? How?

GETTING INFORMATION FROM ILLUSTRATIONS

A. For each of these sentences, write its number on the line under the illustration that matches it best.

1. Hello!

2. I don't know.

3. Nice to meet you.

4. I'm so happy to see you. It's been so long!

5. Everything is great. OK!

6. I'm really worried.

—————   —————   —————

—————   —————   —————

B. Describe how each person(s) is communicating. Name what part(s) of the body that person is using.

1. Would you use the same body language to communicate that message or not?

2. What body language would you use?

C. Work with a partner. Take turns talking about each illustration. Tell as much as you can.

Understanding and Exploring Reading

PREVIEWING THE TITLES

■ READING TIP: *The titles can contain the important ideas of a reading.*

Look at the titles in the reading. Check (✔) the titles that you find in the following list.

_____ Eyes _____ Legs

_____ Ears _____ Body

_____ Hands _____ Head

_____ Arms

Now read the article and find out a few facts about some of the ways we use our bodies to communicate.

What Language Does Our Body Speak?

Body language isn't a language of words in English, Spanish, Arabic, or Japanese. It is a language without words. Body language isn't verbal; it's nonverbal. People communicate nonverbally in many ways. What are some of the important ways people communicate with body language? Is body language the same all over the world, or does it change from one culture to another?

Head

Let's start with the head. Most people around the world nod their heads up and down to mean "yes" or "I agree with you" and side to side to mean "no." These are almost universal signs. Maybe people first communicated with these signs thousands of years ago.

Eyes

Our eyes communicate meaning. But people from different countries communicate differently with their eyes. In North America, it is important to look into the eyes of the person you are talking to. But if you look for more than a few seconds, people will think that you are staring. Staring is impolite. People will ask themselves, "Why is that person staring at me?" In other countries, such as England or Israel, it is usually polite to look for a longer time at the person you are talking to. It shows you are interested in talking to the person.

Hands

We often use our hands to communicate. In many countries, people greet each other with a handshake. In North America, the custom is to take the other person's hand tightly. But in the

Middle East, the custom is to take the other person's hand gently. All over the world, people wave their hands to say hello or goodbye. But people wave differently in different countries.

We can use hand signals to send a short message. But we need to be careful. We don't want to send the wrong message and cause a misunderstanding. In North America, for example, people make a circle with their thumb and forefinger to say "OK" or "Very good." In France, that hand signal has the opposite meaning. And in South American countries, that signal is an insult! In Japan, it is the symbol for money.

The Whole Body

We show emotion nonverbally with our whole body. We open our arms to show welcome or to hug someone. We turn away from someone we disagree with. People tap their feet or their fingers. This shows that they feel angry or impatient. When we feel comfortable, our bodies look relaxed. When we feel uncomfortable, our bodies look tense and nervous.

Body language has a lot to say, but it doesn't use words.

UNDERSTANDING DETAILS

A. Circle the letter of the correct answer. In the reading, underline the words that support your answer. In the margin of the reading, write the question number.

1. Body language is a
   a. verbal language.
   b. nonverbal language.

2. Most people move their heads _____ to mean yes.
   a. side to side
   b. up and down

3. In North America, it is _____ to look into the eyes of the person you are talking to.
   a. important
   b. not important

4. In North America, it is _____ to look at a person for more than a few seconds.
   a. polite
   b. impolite

5. In the Middle East, it is the custom to greet people with a _____ handshake.
   a. gentle
   b. strong

6. We use hand signals to send a _____ message.
   a. long
   b. short

7. We open our arms to someone to show that we _____ them.
   a. welcome
   b. disagree with

8. The meaning of body language is _____ everywhere.
   a. the same
   b. not the same

B. Complete the statements with the correct information from the reading.

1. In North America, if you look at someone for more than a few seconds, people will think that _____ _____ _____.

2. In many countries, people greet each other with _____ _____.

3. People make a circle with their thumb and forefinger.

    a. In North America, it means _____.

    b. In France, it means _____.

    c. In South American countries, it is _____.

    d. In Japan, it is the sign for _____.

Work with a partner. Take turns reading the completed answers to each other. Refer to the reading if you have different answers.

MATCHING IDEAS AND DETAILS

Match the activity with some part of the body.

Parts of the Body	Message/Action
_____ 1. Arms	a. Say "no."
_____ 2. Hands	b. Look at the person you are talking to.
_____ 3. Eyes	c. Say "I agree with you" or "yes."
_____ 4. Head	d. Greet for the first time a person you don't know.
	e. Say "OK" or "That's great."
	f. Say "Goodbye."
	g. Give someone a hug.

Work with a partner. Make a question to ask your partner for information. For example, you can ask your partner, "What kind of message(s) can you give with your eyes?" or "What can you do with your eyes?" Take turns asking and answering questions.

After Reading

REACTING TO THE READING

How do you send these messages nonverbally? Show what part(s) of the body you use and how you communicate your message.

Message/Emotion	Body Language	How to Communicate
Hello.		
Come here.		
It's good to see you.		
Sorry.		
Call me later.		
I'm angry.		
I'm surprised.		
You're late.		
Watch out.		
Don't come here.		
Come here quickly.		
Are you talking to me?		
I have a headache.		

Work with a partner or a small group to show how to use body language to send your messages.

SOLVING A PROBLEM: APPLYING THE INFORMATION

Think about the ideas in the chapter reading. What kinds of problems could people in the following situations have?

Step 1:   Discuss the situation with a partner. Decide what possible problems these people could have.

Step 2:   Think of some possible actions that would show how to solve the situation so that the people feel comfortable. Try to agree on what you would say or do.

1. A student from country X is meeting a fellow student from country Y for the first time. Student X puts out his hand to greet student Y. Student Y looks uncomfortable.

2. A student is 20 minutes late for her appointment with her professor. The professor is sitting tensely at her desk and is tapping her pencil on the desktop.

3. You are walking with two classmates. One classmate, a young woman, sees a young man who is a good friend. She hasn't seen him for a long time and gives him a big hug. Your other friend looks away.

4. You are working with a group of people. Someone makes a hand signal that you don't understand to another person.

5. You are talking with a young woman but are not looking directly into her eyes. You are not sure whether she understands you.

Step 3:   Work with a small group. Compare your ideas. Take turns talking about each situation. Discuss some of the ways to resolve the problem.

Step 4:   Present to the whole class your group's explanation and solution for each situation.

Vocabulary Building

VOCABULARY IN CONTEXT

Complete each sentence with one of the nouns from the following list. Use the words in boldface to help you choose your answer.

a. countries   b. customs   c. handshake   d. head

e. hug   f. signal

1. People around the world nod their _____ **up and down to mean "yes" and side to side to mean "no."**

2. And in **South American** _____, that signal is an insult.

3. She used a special hand _____ to send **a quick message** to her friend.

4. People **greet each other** with a _____.

5. In the Middle East, the _____ for greeting people are **different from those in North America.**

6. She **opened her arms** to give her friend a big _____.

Check your answers. Work with a partner and take turns reading the completed sentences.

CATEGORIZING

Circle the word that does not belong in each of the following groups. Prepare to explain the reason for your choice.

1. head   hand   people   fingers

2. North America   South America   Middle East   England

3. signal   message   sign   eyes

4. hug   thumb   tap   wave

5. hello   goodbye   OK   handshake

6. tense   nervous   interested   angry

Pair Work: Tell your answer and the reason why it doesn't belong.

Expanding Your Language

SPEAKING

Questionnaire: Answer these questions. Be ready to explain your answers. Interview two classmates and ask for their answers to these questions.

1. Is it easy or difficult to understand nonverbal language? Why?

2. Can you use body language to tell people that you agree or disagree with them? How?

3. Can you show people nonverbally that you are happy to see them? How?

4. When you are working in a group, can you signal people that you want to speak? How?

5. Do people from different cultures have different ways of using body language?

6. Is it easy or difficult to learn the nonverbal language of another culture? Why or why not?

Pair Work: Take turns telling the answers you received.

WRITING

Personal Writing: Write six to ten sentences about how you use nonverbal language when you communicate. You can use some of the ideas from this chapter. You can describe some special nonverbal signals you use. Follow these steps:

1. Think of ideas you want to write about. Some ideas could include special body language people use in your country, the way that body language can communicate ideas more easily than words do, or why it is important to "read" body language.

2. Write a list of all the ideas you want to include. Think of the details or examples you have to explain your ideas.

3. Use these ideas to help guide your writing.

4. Write your ideas in complete sentences.

Communication Across Cultures

Chapter Openers

QUESTIONNAIRE: WHEN DO YOU USE ENGLISH?

A. Answer these questions for yourself. Then ask them to two other classmates.

Questions	Yes	No	Sometimes
1. Do you use English when you			
a. talk to friends?			
b. go shopping for food?			
c. go out to listen to music?			
d. read magazines or newspapers?			
e. go to the movies?			
f. go to a party?			
g. are at home?			
h. go shopping for clothes?			
2. Do you ever speak your native language and English mixed together when you			
a. talk with friends?			
b. talk with family?			
c. talk at work?			
d. shop for food or clothes?			

B. Now answer these questions about celebrations.

1. What are some special celebrations you have during the year?

2. What food do you make for these celebrations?

Celebration	*Food*
Example: Thanksgiving	Turkey and pumpkin pie (United States)
Birthday	Cake and ice cream (United States)

a. _____   _____

b. _____   _____

c. _____   _____

PAIRED READINGS

These are two stories about the lives of some people who live in the United States but whose first language is not English. One story is about neighbors who live in the same apartment building but speak different languages. The other story is about bilingual people who mix English and Spanish. What questions could you ask about the daily experiences and lifestyles of people who speak languages other than English? Here is an example.

Question: When do people speak their second language?
Answer: When they are at work.
　　　　　When they are at school.
　　　　　When they are at the supermarket.

■ *READING TIP: Asking questions before reading is a good strategy for helping you to understand more about the subject of the reading. Some important question words are who, what, where, when, and how.*

Write three questions of your own.

1. _____

2. _____

3. _____

Choose one of the stories to read. Work with a person who is reading the same story.

Reading 1: Twelve Languages in One Apartment Building

UNDERSTANDING DETAILS

Read each paragraph and then answer the questions. In the paragraph, underline the words that support your answers.

A. Casa Heiwa is the name of an apartment building in downtown Los Angeles. The name comes from the Spanish word "casa," for house, and the Japanese word "heiwa," for harmony, or peace. Casa Heiwa is a special place to live. People who live in this apartment building speak twelve different languages. In the building are signs in five main languages—Japanese, Chinese, Korean, Spanish, and English—for exits and what to do in case of fire. At building meetings, people communicate in six languages because both Mandarin and Cantonese Chinese are used. The other languages people speak are Vietnamese, Indonesian, Laotian, Tagalog, Thai, and Zapotec.

1. What is Casa Heiwa?

2. Where is it located?

3. Why is Casa Heiwa special?

4. What does Casa Heiwa mean in English?

_____

5. How many languages do people use at building meetings?

_____

B.   People learn from one another about different traditions and different customs. Trying food from other cultures is one of the exciting exchanges that people shared. The apartment building managers plan parties for special celebrations at the building. On the Fourth of July, people bring their own traditional food to the apartment party. Korean families bring *kimchi*, and the South American families bring dishes of roasted peppers. At Thanksgiving, the building managers bring a traditional turkey to every family. Each family cooks the turkey in its own way. Families from Central America cook the turkey in orange juice. One Asian family cooks it like a Chinese-style duck. People learn to eat new foods and to enjoy other new customs, such as traditional music and dances, that they learn from one another. Everyone says that Casa Heiwa is a good place to live.

_____

1. What do people learn from one another?

a. _____

b. _____

2. What parties do the managers plan for?

_____

3. What kind of food do families from different cultures bring on the Fourth of July?

    Cultures   *Food*

    _____   _____

    _____   _____

4. What do the managers bring at Thanksgiving?

    _____

5. What do families from different countries do at Thanksgiving?

    _____

6. Why does everyone think that Casa Heiwa is a good place to live?

    _____

Work with a partner. Take turns reading the questions and answers. Refer to the reading if you have different answers.

RECAPPING THE STORY

■ *RETELLING TIP: Use the illustrations to help you remember and explain the details of the story. Show your partner the illustration as you are explaining. Explain as much as you can.*

Reread the first paragraph quickly. Cover the information and tell your partner as much as you can remember. Ask for help if you forget or give incorrect information. Ask your partner to retell the information. Take turns reading and retelling the information in both paragraphs.

REACTING TO THE STORY

Share your ideas about these questions with a partner.

1. Would you like to live in a place like Casa Heiwa, where people speak many different languages and share their different customs? What are the good and bad points of this type of experience?

2. The story names the foods that people from different cultures prepared. What other customs could people learn from one another?

■ ■
_____

Reading 2: Speaking "Spanglish" in Nueva York

UNDERSTANDING DETAILS

Read each paragraph and then answer the questions. In the paragraph, underline the words that support your answers.

A.   In New York City, two young Hispanic women are talking at lunch. Each woman speaks Spanish perfectly. Each speaks English perfectly. And they both speak Spanglish. Spanglish is a mixture of the two languages. How do people make up words in Spanglish? Take an English word, such as *rave* (an all-night dance and music event popular among young people), and put a Spanish-sounding ending on it. This is called borrowing. Another thing people do is to take an easy word in English, such as *parking,* and use it in a Spanish sentence. This is called switching. People say that Spanglish is easy and that it's fun to speak and to understand if you're bilingual.

_____

1. What languages do these women speak?

   a. _____

   b. _____

2. What is Spanglish?

   _____

3. What is borrowing?

_____

4. What is switching?

_____

5. What two things do people who speak Spanglish say about their experience?

    a. _____

    b. _____

B.   Spanglish is very popular in New York City, Miami, and Los Angeles. These cities have large Spanish-speaking populations. In these cities, you can hear Spanglish on the community radio stations. Some young musicians write songs that have Spanglish words. Where can you find written Spanglish? You can find Spanglish in popular magazines, novels, and poetry. People like to use Spanglish for various reasons. One man says that it just sounds better. One woman says that when she's speaking English, she sometimes uses a Spanish word because it expresses her feelings better than English does. It's easier to talk about such emotions as joy, anger, or love. People say that Spanglish helps them to express their identity as both Spanish and American. It's creative, and it fits their lives today.

_____

1. Where is Spanglish popular?

_____

2. Where can you hear Spanglish?

   _____

3. Where is Spanglish written?

   _____

4. What are three reasons people say they use Spanglish?

   a. _____

   b. _____

   c. _____

5. Which emotions does one woman say are easier to talk about in Spanglish?

   _____

RECAPPING THE STORY

■ **RETELLING TIP:** *Use the illustrations to help you remember and explain the details of the story. Show your partner the illustration as you are explaining. Explain as much as you can.*

Reread the first paragraph quickly. Cover the information and tell your partner as much as you can remember. Use the illustrations to help you. Ask for help if you forget or give incorrect information. Ask your partner to retell the information. Take turns reading and telling the information in both paragraphs.

REACTING TO THE STORY

1. Do you ever mix the words from two languages or speak both at the same time? Explain when and why.

2. How do you feel when you combine words from two languages when you are talking?

After Reading

COMPARING THE STORIES

A. Work with a partner(s) who read a different story. Tell your partner the details of the story. Use the illustrations to help you tell the story. Then listen to your partner's story.

B. Together, complete this task. Circle *T* for true and *F* for false. If the statement is false, give the correct information.

1. T   F   People who live at Casa Heiwa speak ten different languages.

2. T   F   People all over the world speak Spanglish.

3. T   F   At Casa Heiwa, people don't celebrate any holidays together.

4. T   F   People use Spanglish when they talk, write, and sing.

5. T   F   At Casa Heiwa, the building managers bring people turkey at Christmas.

6. T   F   People use Spanglish only when they feel angry.

C. Circle the statement you think is true for both stories.

1. People can use their first language and their second language together.

2. People cannot keep their own traditions when they live in another country.

3. People can learn new customs and languages, enjoy them, and make them their own.

D. Discuss the "Reacting to the Story" questions for both stories. Explain your answers as much as possible.

Vocabulary Building

VOCABULARY IN CONTEXT

In written English, ideas are often presented in an organized way. First, a sentence presents a general idea. Then the next sentence has a specific detail or example. Here is one example of this kind of organization from the story.

People bring their traditional food to the party. Korean families bring
(General)   (Details)
kimchi, and the South American families bring dishes of roasted
(Details)

peppers.

A. Look back at the readings in this chapter and find three more examples of this pattern. Write them on the lines below.

General	*Specific*
1. a. _____	b. _____
2. a. _____	b. _____
3. a. _____	b. _____

B. Complete each sentence with one of the verbs from the list. Use the words in boldface to help you choose your answer.

a. bring   b. communicate   c. enjoy   d. hear   e. speak

f. understand   g. use

1. They _____ learning new customs and they **have fun** eating food from different countries.

2. They **talk** in Spanglish to _____ their feelings to one another.

3. In many cities, you can _____ Spanglish **songs on the radio**.

4. I _____ in my first language **when I talk to my family**.

5. How many **languages** do you _____ at home?

6. I asked people to _____ some food for everyone to share **when they come to the party**.

7. I _____ the language because I **learned it in school**.

Check your answers. Work with a partner and read the completed sentences.

CATEGORIZING

Based on the chapter readings and information of your own, complete the following chart with words that belong in the categories.

Countries/Regions	Languages Spoken	Traditional Foods
Example: United States	English	Turkey at Thanksgiving
1. _____	_____	_____
2. _____	_____	_____
3. _____	_____	_____
4. _____	_____	_____
5. _____	_____	_____

Options: Interview your class members and complete this chart with information from the other students. List as many ideas as you can.

Expanding Your Language

SPEAKING

A. Answer these questions for yourself. Then interview two people in your class. Ask them to answer these questions.

You	Student A	Student B
1. What different languages can you speak? a. b. c.	a. b. c.	a. b. c.
2. What languages do you use a. at home? b. at school? c. at work? d. with friends?	a. b. c. d.	a. b. c. d.
3. What are your favorite activities in a. reading? *poetry* b. listening? *music* c. talking? *talking to friends* d. writing? *letters to my parents*	a. b. c. d.	a. b. c. d.

B. Tell the information from your interviews to other people in the class. Find out who

1. speaks the most languages.

   _____

2. uses English at home.

   _____

3. likes to listen to music.

   _____

4. likes to watch movies.

   _____

5. likes to read stories.

   _____

6. likes to read poetry.

   _____

7. likes to write letters.

   _____

8. likes to talk to people.

   _____

C. Report to the class what you found out.

WRITING

1. Think about reading and speaking in your first language and in English. How do they compare? Write about one of the following topics:

a. What makes reading and speaking easier or more enjoyable in your first language and in English?

b. How many languages do you hear or see in your daily life? Give examples of when you can find more than one language being used, such as signs in airports or government offices.

2. Explain to a partner what you wrote about your topic.

Leave Me a Message

Chapter Openers

CATEGORIZING

1. Choose Set A below or Set B in the Exercise Pages section at the end of the book. Student A works with the messages below. Student B works with the messages in Set B, in the exercise on page E-1.

2. Read the messages and decide what category they best belong in. Write *W* for work, *S* for school, and *H* for home. Some messages might fit in more than one category.

SET A

a. _____ Harry needs your final weekly report today.

b. _____ Don't forget to put out the garbage.

c. _____ We need salsa for the party. Get some on the way home.

d. _____ The librarian called. Your book is overdue. Bring it in tomorrow.

3. Work with a partner to check your answers.

4. Work with a partner who chose the messages in Set B. Take turns reading to each other the messages in both Set A and Set B. Decide which categories your partner's messages belong in.

5. Write a message of your own for the following people:

Friend: _____

Classmate: _____

Family member: _____

Teacher: _____

Work with a partner to give the messages you wrote.

DISCUSSION QUESTIONS

Think about these questions. Share your ideas with a partner or with a small group.

1. What is a Post-it Note? Describe what it looks like.

2. What kind of messages can you write on a Post-it Note?

3. When do you use these notes?

4. Why are Post-it Notes useful?

Exploring and Understanding Reading

MATCHING

Write the letter of the caption that matches the pictures.

 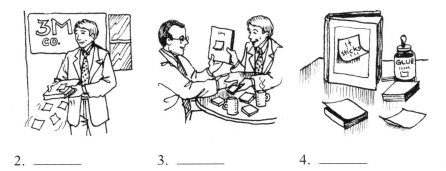

1. _____   2. _____   3. _____   4. _____

CAPTIONS

a. He needed a bookmark that wouldn't fall out of the book.

b. He put glue on the back edge of the paper. The glue stuck to the pages of the book.

c. He wrote a question on the sticky paper and put it on a report. His boss took the note, wrote an answer, and sent it back.

d. The two men had coffee to celebrate the invention of Post-it Notes.

PREDICTING

■ *READING TIP:*
Predicting the kind of information you might find in a reading will make it easier for you to understand what you read.

The following reading is about Post-it Notes. What do you think you could learn about from this reading? Check (✔) the information you expect to find in the story.

1. _____ How Post-it Notes were invented

2. _____ Where you can buy Post-it Notes

3. _____ Various uses for Post-it Notes

4. _____ The price of Post-it Notes

Now read the story and put a check beside the ideas that you find.

Notes for Anyone, Anywhere, Anytime

A. Every day, we have messages to give people. Do you want to tell people about an important meeting? Do you have to leave your office for 5 minutes? Do you want to remember something important? Write the information on a Post-it Note. Post-it Notes have a special glue on the edge of the paper. They are sticky so that you can leave them anywhere—on a door or on a wall or in a book—and they won't fall out. You can reuse the notes because they have special glue on the back. If you take off the note and put it back down, it will stay in place.

B. Who invented Post-it Notes? Art Fry was a scientist who worked for the famous 3M Company. He needed a bookmark that stayed in place but didn't tear the page. A friend at the company was making special glue. Fry took some of the glue and put it on the back of a yellow piece of paper. Then he wrote a report to his boss and put the yellow sticky paper on the top page. His boss took off the note, wrote an answer, stuck the paper back on, and sent it back. The two men met for coffee in the cafeteria that afternoon. Fry's boss congratulated him on his invention. This was the beginning of Post-it Notes.

C. Today, everyone uses them for many different purposes. One man used it to write a marriage proposal. He wrote, "Will you marry me?" and put the Post-it Note on his girlfriend's front door. She wrote her answer and put the note back on his door. One mother put a note on the back of her son's car before he left on a long trip. When he arrived, he found the note. After 3,000 miles, it was still on the car. There are Post-it Notes to suit everyone's tastes. You can buy Post-it Notes in eighteen different colors, twenty-seven different sizes, and fifty-six different shapes. Post-it Notes are popular around the world.

UNDERSTANDING DETAILS

A. Circle the letter of the correct answer. In the reading, underline the words that support your answer.

1. People use Post-it Notes for
   a. writing long messages.
   b. writing reports.
   c. writing short messages.

2. You can put a Post-it Note
   a. almost anywhere.
   b. only in books.
   c. only on a wall.

3. Post-it Notes
    a. can be reused.
    b. can't be reused.
    c. can sometimes be reused.

4. Post-it Notes
    a. will stay in place.
    b. will stay in place for a short time.
    c. won't stay in place.

5. Art Fry
    a. made the glue for Post-it Notes.
    b. used the glue a friend made.
    c. made the glue with a friend.

6. Post-it Notes
    a. come in only one color, size, and shape.
    b. come in only a few colors, sizes, and shapes.
    c. come in many colors, sizes, and shapes.

B. Complete the following statements. In the reading, underline information that supports your answer.

1. One man used a Post-it Note to write a _____

   _____ .

2. A mother put a note on the back of _____

   _____ _____ .

3. Art Fry was _____ _____ at 3M.

4. He wrote _____ _____ to his boss and put a note

   _____ _____ _____ page.

5. Today, Post-it Notes are _____ all over _____

   _____ .

Work with a partner. Take turns reading the questions and answers to each other. Refer to the reading if you have different answers.

After Reading

APPLYING THE INFORMATION

A. Matching: Use the information from the reading and ideas of your own to match the questions in Column A with the answers in Column B.

Column A

_____ 1. Where and when do you want to meet?

_____ 2. What do you want to talk about?

_____ 3. Can you meet with me today?

_____ 4. Can you ask Jim to make more of that glue?

_____ 5. What do you think the company will say?

Column B

a. Sure, I'm free this afternoon.

b. 3:00 in the cafeteria.

c. I think they'll say that you've invented something very interesting.

d. I've got an idea for a useful new product.

e. Sure, let's call him right away.

Now write the sequence of questions and answers in the correct order on the lines below.

1. _____

2. _____

3. _____

4. _____

5. _____

B. Delivering a Message: Two messages were sent to each member of the Armstrong family: John, who is a painter; Nancy, forty-nine, a doctor; Mona, twenty-one, a dancer; and Sam, nineteen, a college student. Work with a partner. Together, read your messages and decide whose box they belong in.

_____ 1. Hi, Dad. I'll be home at 6:00 P.M. Hold supper for me.

_____ 2. Mrs. Brown called. Her arm still hurts. Can you see her? The number is 555-8976.

_____ 3. You have a rehearsal at 8:00. Meet Joe at the studio.

_____ 4. Bob called. He wants you to call him about the test.

_____ 5. Don't worry about supper. I'll pick up a pizza on the way home.

_____ 6. The test is postponed. It won't be until next week.

_____ 7. Don't forget to bring your music to the rehearsal.

_____ 8. The hospital called. The operation will be at 9:00.

Make your own message for each member of the Armstrong family. Write messages for John and Nancy here. Write messages for Mona and Sam on the next page.

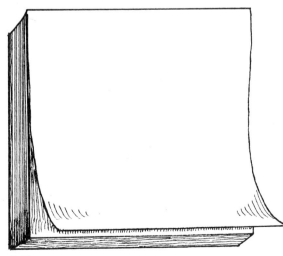

John

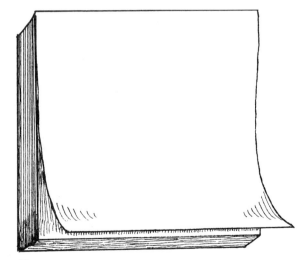

Nancy

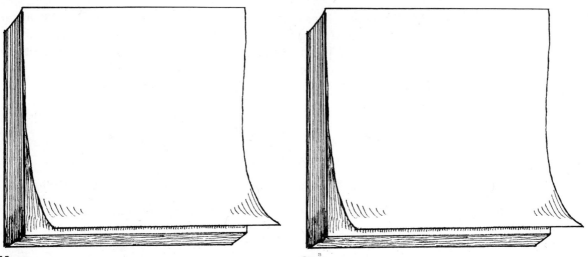

Mona   *Sam*

Vocabulary Building

VOCABULARY IN CONTEXT

Complete each sentence with one of the verbs from the following list. Use the words in boldface to help you choose your answer.

a. buy   b. leave   c. put   d. remember   e. use   f. write

1. He ——————— the note **on the top of** the report.

2. Did you ——————— to go to the meeting, or **did you forget**?

3. You can ——————— the notes **in any store** anywhere around the world.

4. He needed **a pen** to ——————— a note for her to read.

5. Can you ——————— the note in a place **where she will find it**?

6. Can you ——————— these papers, **or should I throw them away**?

PREPOSITIONS

Write the preposition that best completes the following sentences.

a. in   b. of   c. off   d. on   e. out   f. for

1. You should take _____ the note after you read the report.

2. Write the message and leave it _____ the door.

3. Put the note _____ where he will see it.

4. Put the note _____ my office door.

5. I'm busy now, but can I speak to you _____ 5 minutes?

6. I asked her to bring me a box _____ copies _____ the office.

VERBS: PRESENT AND PAST

Write the past form of the following verbs. Circle these words in the reading.

1. invent _____   2. need _____

3. take _____   4. write _____

5. stick _____   6. meet _____

Check your answers. Write three sentences and three questions of your own, using both the present and past forms of any of these verbs.

Expanding Your Language

SPEAKING

Role Play: Work with a partner. Choose the role of one of the main characters in this reading, such as Art Fry and his boss or the young man and his fiancée. Together, write out the conversation between the two people, based on the reading and on ideas of your own.

Here is one example of how to begin the conversation:

Art: Hi, Jim. I have an idea that I'm working on. I want to talk to you about it. Do you have time to see me?
Jim: Sure, let's go for coffee.

WRITING

Topic Writing: Based on the reading and the other activities in this chapter, prepare to write ten to twelve sentences about the invention and use of Post-it Notes. To do this, make an outline for the ideas you could write about. Here is a sample outline:

A. What a Post-it Note is
  1. What it looks like (color, size, and so on)
  2. What is special about it

B. Many different uses for a Post-it Note
  1. Leave a reminder to yourself
  2. Leave a special message for others
  3. A funny example

C. The invention of Post-it Notes
  1. Who
  2. Reason
  3. How successful it is

1. Write two or three sentences about each idea in your outline. Remember that in written English, a general idea is given in one sentence, and the following sentences give details or examples. Refer to page 21 for some examples of this writing.

2. Use your outline to write the information in complete sentences.

3. Work with a partner. Explain to each other the information that you wrote about.

4. Give the writing to your teacher.

Read On: Taking It Further

Researchers have found that the more you read, the more your vocabulary will increase and the more you will understand. A good knowledge of vocabulary will help you to do well in school and in business.

To find out more about making reading a habit for yourself, answer the following questionnaire.

READING QUESTIONNAIRE

Rank the activities that you think help you to increase the language you understand. Write *1* beside those that help you the most to learn new language, *2* beside those that help you the second most, and so on. If you find two activities that help you equally, write the same number.

_____ Memorizing word lists

_____ Reading texts that are assigned for class

_____ Reading texts that I choose for myself

_____ Talking about the texts that we read for class

_____ Talking about the texts that I choose for myself

_____ Learning how to guess the meaning of words that are new

_____ Doing vocabulary exercises for class reading

_____ Doing extra vocabulary exercises for homework

_____ Studying the dictionary to find out the parts of words

_____ Using the dictionary to look up new words I don't understand

Discuss your questionnaire with a partner. Do not change your answers. Explain the reasons for your rankings and your experiences with reading. Are there other activities that help you to increase your vocabulary? Explain what these are and how they help you.

READING JOURNAL

■ *TIP:* *Keep a note-book to write entires for your reading journal and vocabulary log.*

An important way to improve your reading skills and to increase your vocabulary is to find material that you choose to read. This activity is called "reading for pleasure." Here are some ideas to start you out.

Find some readings on the topics in this unit that you are interested in and that are at your level. Your teacher can help you to find some stories to read for your pleasure. For example, you could choose an easy-reading edition of the life story of Thomas Edison, the inventor of the lightbulb. You could also read the story of Helen Keller, who learned to communicate even though she was blind and deaf.

Another source of reading material is the magazine and newspaper section of your bookstore or library. Discuss with others in a small group what you would like to read. Your group members could recommend something good for you to read. Try to work with a reading partner. Select a reading that your partner or partners will read as well. Make a schedule for the times when you plan to do your personal reading and a time when you would like to finish.

SPEAKING

Be ready to talk with a partner or with others in a small group about what you read. You can complete the following form by writing some sentences to help you remember what is important for the others to know.

READING JOURNAL

Write the following information in your journal entry:

Title of the reading: _____

Author: _____

Subject of the reading: _____

_____

Who are the important people in the story?

1. _____

2. _____

3. _____

4. _____

5. _____

What are some of the important ideas?

1. _____

2. _____

3. _____

4. _____

5. _____

Recommendation

This is or isn't good to read, because: _____

1. _____

2. _____

3. _____

4. _____

5. _____

VOCABULARY LOG

Choose five important words that you learned from each chapter. Write the words and a definition in your notebook. Check your definition with the teacher.

Chapter 1	*Word*	*Definition*
1.	benefits	some good points
2.		
3.		
4.		
5.		

On a separate page in your notebook, write five sentences. In each sentence, use one of the words you chose.

UNIT 2

The Mysteries of Sleep

Sleep is a reward for some, a punishment for others.

—Isidore Ducasse

Introducing the Topic

We all need to sleep, but getting a good night's sleep is not easy for everyone. This unit introduces some ideas and questions about sleep. Chapter 4 shows us that many people today are not getting enough sleep. Why does this happen, and what problems does this cause? In Chapter 5, you'll read about the stories of two people and their personal experiences with their sleep problems. You'll find out how sleep problems affect the people's lives. Chapter 6 presents some interesting facts about the subject of dreams.

Points of Interest

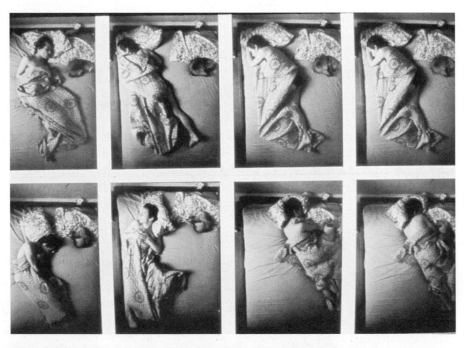

What kind of sleep problem do you think this person is having?

Sleep: How Much Is Not Enough?

Chapter Openers

QUESTIONNAIRE

Answer these questions for yourself. Ask two classmates these same questions.

Questions	You	Student A	Student B
1. How many hours a day do you need to sleep?			
2. What time do you a. get up? b. go to bed?	a. b.	a. b.	a. b.
3. What activities do you do a. in the morning? b. in the afternoon? c. in the evening?	a. b. c.	a. b. c.	a. b. c.
4. Check (✓) the time(s) of the day you feel really tired	( ) in the morning ( ) in the afternoon ( ) in the evening	( ) in the morning ( ) in the afternoon ( ) in the evening	( ) in the morning ( ) in the afternoon ( ) in the evening
5. How many hours of sleep does a person need as a(n)	baby _____ teenager _____ adult _____ older adult _____	baby _____ teenager _____ adult _____ older adult _____	baby _____ teenager _____ adult _____ older adult _____

Tell the information from your interviews to another person in class.

■ Understanding and Exploring Reading

PREVIEWING

To preview, follow these steps:

1. Read the title and the first and last sentences of each paragraph in the story.

2. Based on that information, check (✔) from the following list the ideas you expect to find out about in this reading.

I expect to find out

1. _____ why sleep is important to our health.

2. _____ some stories about people with sleep problems.

3. _____ why more people are not getting enough sleep.

4. _____ how the need for sleep changes as we get older.

5. _____ what kinds of sleep problems are difficult to solve.

With a partner, compare your choices. Try to agree on your answers. Then read all of the paragraphs. See whether you should change any of the choices you made.

■■ ――――――

Sleeping Less in the Twenty-First Century

A.   Today, people are getting less sleep than they need. We need to get 8 hours of sleep each night. But today, many of us are not getting enough hours of sleep. People take time from sleep to do other things. People work longer, go to meetings at night, eat supper late, go food shopping, watch television, spend hours on line, or go out until late. Some people wake up early to go to the gym, do housework, study, or cook food for later in the day. In today's society, it is easier to do more at night. Stores stay open 24 hours a day for shopping. Companies want their employees to work late. Television stations broadcast all day and all night. People can stay up to watch any time. There are many reasons that people today are not getting the sleep they need.

B.   Getting enough sleep is important to your health. When you sleep, your body produces chemicals called hormones. These hormones help the body to rest and to keep healthy. If you don't get enough sleep, your memory will not work well. You will feel worried and in a bad mood. The body uses sleep to make energy for itself. Without enough sleep, you feel tired. When you lose sleep, your body ages at a faster rate. Sleeping reduces the effects of aging.

C.   Our need to sleep changes as we get older. Newborn babies sleep from 16–20 hours a day. Teenagers need about 9 or 10 hours of sleep. Adults need about 8 hours, and the elderly need about 6 or 7. As we age, we lose our ability to sleep. We don't sleep as long or as deeply. Older people can spend a lot of time in bed. But they don't sleep well. It takes them longer to fall asleep, and they don't fall into a deep sleep. Deep sleep is the sleep that refreshes our bodies. Sleep problems can be serious. People with serious sleep problems might need to see a doctor or to change their lifestyles.

UNDERSTANDING DETAILS

A. Circle the letter of the correct answer. In the reading, underline the words that support your answer.

1. People are getting
   a. more sleep than they need.
   b. less sleep than they need.

2. People are doing
   a. more things at night than in the past.
   b. fewer things at night than in the past.

3. Stores stay open
   a. a few hours at night.
   b. all night.

4. When you don't get enough sleep,
   a. your body doesn't produce hormones it needs.
   b. your body produces the hormones it needs.

5. If you don't get enough sleep, you will
   a. remember better and feel happier.
   b. not remember as well or feel as happy.

6. Older people

   a. spend more time in bed but sleep less.
   b. spend less time in bed but sleep more.

B. Complete the following sentences. Underline the information that supports your answer.

1. Today, people _____ longer, go to _____,

   eat late, and go _____ shopping.

2. People wake up early to go to the _____, do

   _____, study, or _____ food.

3. Your body produces _____ that help you to

   _____ and keep _____.

4. When you _____ sleep, your _____ ages.

5. When we get older, we don't get as much _____ sleep.

Work with a partner. Take turns reading the answers. Refer to the reading if you have different answers.

After Reading

APPLYING THE INFORMATION: PROBLEM SOLVING

Use the information from the reading and from your own experience to give advice that could solve the following problems. Give as much information in your advice as possible. Include details about how to find time during the day and week, or how to make changes to their schedules. Make a list of ideas to discuss with others.

1. Alice has a full-time job. She works from 8 A.M. to 4 P.M. She is a single mother with two young children. She studies part time in the evening. She feels tired and can't concentrate during the day.

   What is Alice's problem? What are some possible solutions to her problems?

   _____

   _____

   _____

2. Paul is an active university student who does well in school and takes part in a lot of other school activities. He usually goes to bed late and gets up at 7:00 A.M. to get the bus to be in school on time. Lately, he's been spending a lot of his time on line, chatting with his friends and discovering some exciting Web sites. He's staying up later and later. He says that he feels tired most mornings and has even started to miss his bus.

What is Paul's problem? What are some possible ways Paul could solve his problems?

_____

_____

_____

With a partner or with others in a small group, share the list of ideas you made. Present your solutions to the whole class.

Vocabulary Building

VOCABULARY IN CONTEXT

A. Complete each statement with one of the nouns from the following list. Use the words in boldface to help you choose your answer.

a. ability   b. elderly   c. employees   d. energy

e. memory   f. mood   g. teenagers

1. It takes a lot of _____ **to work all day**.

2. **As we age**, we lose our _____ to sleep.

3. Her _____ was so bad that **she couldn't remember** my name.

4. It is **difficult to be with** him when he is in a bad _____.

5. Why do these _____ seem **to sleep all day**: from 2 A.M. until 2 P.M?

6. The _____ have a lot of sleep problems **because of their age**.

7. The **company** asked whether all _____ could **work** until 8 P.M.

B. Decide whether the word underlined in each sentence is a noun or a verb. Circle *N* for noun or *V* for verb.

1. N V We <u>need</u> to get 8 hours sleep.

2. N V Our <u>need</u> to sleep changes as we get older.

3. N V As we <u>age</u>, we lose our ability to sleep.

4. N V It is difficult to tell her <u>age</u>; it could be sixteen or twenty-six.

5. N V I have to get a good night's <u>sleep</u> tonight.

6. N V Can I <u>sleep</u> in the big bedroom?

C. Jigsaw Sentences: Match the beginning of each sentence (Column A) with the ending that fits best (Column B).

Column A

_____ 1. When you sleep

_____ 2. If you don't get enough sleep,

_____ 3. People with serious sleep problems

_____ 4. In today's society,

_____ 5. Getting enough sleep

Column B

a. is important to your health.

b. might need to see a doctor.

c. your body produces hormones.

d. it is easier to do more at night.

e. your memory will not work well.

Check your answers. Work with a partner and take turns reading your answers.

▋ Expanding Your Language

SPEAKING

Questions and Answers: Write five questions about the topic of sleep. Write three questions using question words and two yes/no questions. Use the information in the reading to help find ideas to make your questions. Check your questions with your teacher. Then use your questions to interview two people in class. Ask your questions, and in note form, write the answers you receive.

SAMPLE QUESTIONS
1. Why do teenagers need to sleep more than older people?
2. In the future, will people work longer or shorter hours?
3. When do you feel the most tired?
4. Is it a good idea to take a nap during the day?

Discuss the information from your interviews with others in a small group.

WRITING

Writing Questions and Answers: Write answers to three of the most interesting questions you prepared. Use pages of your own for the writing. Then work with a partner and report the questions and answers you wrote.

CHAPTER 5

Sleep Problems

Chapter Openers

DISCUSSION QUESTIONS: TOSSING AND TURNING

Think about these questions. Share your ideas with a partner or in a small group.

1. Do you ever have trouble sleeping?

2. What do you do when you can't sleep?

3. How do you feel when you don't get enough sleep?

4. What are some kinds of sleep problems?

5. How can people solve their sleep problems?

PAIRED READINGS

These are the stories of two people who are having trouble getting a good night's sleep. They are writing to a newspaper column doctor who gives advice to the newspaper's readers. Read and find out about their problems and what the doctor suggests. Look for the similarities and differences in the stories.

Choose one of the stories to read. Work with a partner who is reading the same story.

■■
_____

Reading 1: One Woman's Story of How Snoring Ruined Her Life

UNDERSTANDING DETAILS

Read each paragraph and then answer the questions. In the paragraph, underline the words that support your answers.

Ann's Problem

A.   Dear Dr. Snow,

My husband, Bob, sleeps very soundly. He gets 8 hours of sleep and wakes up feeling great. He is rested and ready for the day. He is usually in a good mood in the morning. I am not so lucky. I can fall asleep, but then I get only 3 hours of sleep. Why? The reason is that my husband snores. He snores so loudly that it wakes me up. Then I can't get to sleep again. I try to move him onto his side, but after a while, he moves onto his back. Then the snoring begins again. Sometimes, I move to the couch to get some sleep. But often, he is snoring so loudly that I can hear him from the living room. I never get enough sleep.

1. How many hours does Bob sleep?

   _____

2. How does he feel in the morning?

   _____

3. How many hours of sleep does Ann get?

   _____

4. What does Ann's husband do?

   _____

5. What does Ann sometimes do?

   _____

6. What can Ann still hear from the living room?

   _____

B.   When I don't get enough sleep, I am in a bad mood. I feel tired and grumpy when I wake up. I am very sleepy in the afternoon. Yesterday, at work, I was at a very long meeting. There were about twenty people around the table. It felt very hot. I had a headache. I closed my eyes for a moment. The next thing I knew, my boss was calling my name. She looked angry. Did I fall asleep? I was so embarrassed. Now I'm afraid of losing my job. What do I do?

_____

1. How does Ann feel when she wakes up?

   _____

2. How does she feel in the afternoon?

   _____

3. Where was she yesterday?

   _____

4. How did she feel at the meeting?

   _____

5. What happened to her when she closed her eyes?

   _____

6. What is Ann afraid of?

   _____

The Doctor's Answer

C.   Dear Ann,

   To help you and your husband, I need to find out more. Is your husband overweight? Does he smoke? Is he very tired? These are some things that can cause snoring. They aren't good for his health. If the answer to any of these questions is yes, he should change his habits. What about the mattress on your bed? Is it very soft? Get a good, strong mattress to sleep on, and make sure that the room is cool. If this doesn't work, there are other methods, such as surgery or a special breathing mask.

   _____

1. What questions does the doctor ask about Ann's husband?

   a. _____

   b. _____

   c. _____

2. Should Ann's husband change his habits? Why?

   _____

3. What kind of mattress should Ann get to prevent snoring?

   _____

4. What other methods are there to solve the problem of snoring?

   a. _____

   b. _____

Work with a partner. Take turns reading the questions and answers to each other. Refer to the reading if your answers are different.

RECAPPING THE STORY

Reread the first paragraph quickly. Cover the information and tell your partner as much as you can remember. Ask for help if you forget or give incorrect information. Ask your partner to retell the information. Take turns reading and telling the information in all of the paragraphs.

REACTING TO THE STORY

Discuss these questions with a partner.

1. Do you think that Ann might lose her job because of her sleep problem? Why or why not?

2. What do you think that Ann and her husband should do to solve this situation?

Compare your answers with others in a small group. Choose the most interesting answer to present to others in your class.

Reading 2: How Insomnia Changed My Life

UNDERSTANDING DETAILS

Read each paragraph and then answer the questions. In the paragraph, underline the words that support your answers.

Judy's Problem

A.   Dear Dr. Snow,

I'm a thirty-two-year-old single mom with two kids, fourteen and nine years old. I have trouble falling asleep. At night when I get into bed, I start to worry. I worry about the problems I have at work. Most of all, I worry about my children. There are so many things to do for them. I don't have enough time for everything.

1. Give some personal information about Judy:

a. Age: _____

b. Marital status: _____

c. Children: _____

2. What sleep problem does she have?

_____

3. What does she worry about?

_____

_____

4. Why does she worry?

_____

_____

B.   When I can't sleep, I get up and do some housework, or I work on the computer in my bedroom. I get up at 5:30 to have everything ready for the kids: make their breakfast, make their lunches, and get ready for work. Some nights, I get only 2 or 3 hours of sleep. During the day, I drink coffee to stay awake. I need to have coffee almost all the time. Should I take drugs to fall asleep? What do I need to do?

_____

1. What does she do when she can't sleep?

_____

_____

2. At what time does she get up?

_____

3. What does she have to do in the morning?

_____

4. How much sleep does she often get?

_____

5. Why does she drink coffee during the day?

_____

6. What question does she ask herself?

_____

The Doctor's Answer

C.   Dear Judy,

You are not alone. Many women suffer from insomnia because of stress, pain, and other health problems. But don't take drugs to fall asleep. There are other, better remedies. Try relaxation exercises before you go to bed. Don't drink coffee after 1 P.M. Don't work in your bedroom at night. Move your computer to another room. Make your bedroom quiet and comfortable. If you start to worry, write a list of the problems and some possible solutions. Tell yourself that you'll look at the list in the morning. Then relax and go to sleep.

----

1. Why do many women suffer from insomnia?

    _____

2. What shouldn't she do to fall asleep?

    _____

    _____

3. What shouldn't she do in her bedroom?

    _____

    _____

4. What should she do to her bedroom?

    _____

    _____

5. What should she do if she starts to worry?

    _____

    _____

6. What should she tell herself?

    _____

    _____

Work with a partner. Take turns reading the questions and answers to each other. Refer to the reading if you have different answers.

RECAPPING THE STORY

Reread the first paragraph quickly. Then cover the information and tell your partner as much as you can remember. Ask for help if you forget or give incorrect information. Ask your partner to retell the information. Take turns reading and telling the information in all of the paragraphs.

REACTING TO THE STORY

Discuss these questions with a partner.

1. What do you think could be some reasons why more women than men suffer from insomnia?

2. What advice would you give to a friend who has insomnia? What questions would you want to ask?

Compare your answers with others in a small group. Choose the most interesting answer to present to others in your class.

After Reading

COMPARING THE STORIES

A. Work with a partner who read a different story. Tell your partner the details of the story you read. Then listen to your partner's story. With your partner, tell back the story you heard. Finally, discuss the questions in the "Reacting to the Story" section of both readings.

B. Work with a partner. Circle *T* for true or *F* for false. If the answer is false, tell your partner the correct information.

1. T F   Both of the people in these stories have the same sleep problem.

2. T F   Ann and Judy are both married.

3. T F   Ann and Judy both work.

4. T F   Ann and Judy are both worried about their children.

5. T F   Ann and Judy both ask a doctor for advice.

6. T F   Ann and Judy get similar advice for their problems.

SOLVING A PROBLEM: APPLYING THE INFORMATION

Based on the information in the chapter readings and your own ideas, what advice would you give to these people? Follow these steps.

Step 1: Discuss the situation with a partner. What problem does the person have?

Step 2: Make a list of three to five suggestions you could give. Include suggestions about what the person should or could do or not do. For example: You should make sure that the bedroom is quiet and comfortable. You shouldn't drink any coffee at night. You could try to take a nap during the afternoon.

1. Paul, a student from another country, is studying in your class. Paul tells you that he is having a hard time going to bed before 2:00 or 3:00 in the morning. He likes to study late at night and then watches the late-night movie. Sometimes, he watches TV all night. The television is in his bedroom. Then in the morning, he can't get up. Paul wants your advice.

   YOUR ADVICE

   _____

   _____

   _____

   _____

2. Joan is a college student. She works part time to pay for her expenses. She works during the week from 6:00 until 11:00 four nights a week. Joan comes home at around midnight, and then she studies until 3:00 in the morning. On the weekend, she sleeps late to catch up on her sleep. Now her boss has told her that he needs someone to work Saturday and Sunday from 7:00 A.M. until 3:00 P.M. Joan is worried that she won't get enough sleep, but she doesn't want to lose her job. Joan wants your advice.

   YOUR ADVICE

   _____

   _____

   _____

   _____

Vocabulary Building

VOCABULARY IN CONTEXT

Complete each statement with one of the adjectives from the following list. Use the words in boldface to help you choose your answer.

a. angry   b. comfortable   c. embarrassed   d. grumpy

e. health   f. lucky   g. quiet   h. sleepy   i. strong

1. I think he was _____ because **I fell asleep while he was talking**.

2. I asked **the doctor to give me advice** about my

   _____ problems.

3. When you are in **a bad mood**, it makes me feel _____ too.

4. The bed was so soft and _____ that **I fell asleep very quickly**.

5. **No one is at home** today, so the house is very _____.

6. I felt so _____ that I couldn't remember her name **that my face turned red**.

7. He's very _____ that **he can sleep anywhere even if it's noisy**.

8. I like to drink very _____ **coffee when I have to stay awake**.

9. **I stayed up all night**, so today I feel so _____ that I can't study.

JIGSAW SENTENCES

But is a word that introduces a contrasting or a conditional idea. *But* can begin a sentence, or it can join two clauses in a sentence. Use your understanding of the ideas to complete these sentences.

Match the beginning of each sentence (Column A) with the ending that fits best (Column B).

Column A

_____ 1. He tries to sleep on his side,

_____ 2. She wants to go to bed early,

_____ 3. I try not to worry,

_____ 4. She spends a lot of time in bed,

_____ 5. He called her name,

Column B

a. but she didn't hear him.

b. but she doesn't sleep well.

c. but it's difficult to forget about daily problems.

d. but she likes to watch the late movie.

e. but he often moves onto his back.

Check your answers. Work with a partner and take turns reading your answers.

CATEGORIZING

In each of the following groups, circle the word that does not belong. Prepare to explain the reason for your choice.

1. tired   awake   sleepy   grumpy

2. often   mattress   always   sometimes

3. snoring   smoking   cool   worrying

4. stress   pain   headache   coffee

Pair Work: Tell your answer and the reason why it doesn't belong.

Expanding Your Language

SPEAKING

A. Role Play: Work with a partner. Choose the role of one of the people in one of the stories. Based on the ideas in the story and on ideas of your own, write out a conversation. You may want to add characters, such as Ann's husband or boss or Judy's children, to the story.

Here is one example of how to begin the conversation.

Ann: Doctor, I have a terrible problem. My husband wakes me up. He snores and I can't sleep.

Doctor: Well, tell me a little more. How often do you wake up at night?

Use your lines to act out the story, but you do not have to memorize the lines. You can be creative and improvise if you need to.

B. Two-Minute Taped Talk: Record a 2-minute audiotape about one of the stories in this chapter. To make your tape, follow these steps. Choose one of the stories to talk about. Reread the information.

1. In note form, write the information that you remember. Include as many of the important facts of the story as possible.
2. Refer to the reading and check your notes for information that you left out or that was incorrect. Make any necessary changes.
3. Practice telling the story a few times until you can speak without reading what you wrote.
4. Time yourself as you try to speak as clearly and naturally as possible.
5. Record yourself telling the story.
6. Give the tape to your teacher for feedback.

WRITING

Write a sentence of your own, based on the definitions of these sleep expressions.

1. **Sleep in: To get up later than you usually would.** Example: I was up until 2:00 A.M., so I decided to **sleep in** until 11:00 A.M. today.

    _____

    _____

2. **Sleep on: To think about something before doing it.** Example: He wants me to go out with him, but I told him I wanted to **sleep on** it.

    _____

    _____

3. **Sleep over: To spend the night at someone else's home.** Example: She asked five of her friends to **sleep over** at her house after the party.

    _____

    _____

4. **Sleeping bag: A warm, lined bag used to keep warm when sleeping outdoors or away from home.** Example: I brought my **sleeping bag** for the camping trip.

    _____

    _____

CHAPTER 6

Why Do We Dream?

Chapter Openers

DISCUSSION QUESTIONS: THE WORLD OF OUR DREAMS

Think about these questions. Share your ideas with a partner or in a small group.

1. How often do you think you dream?

2. What dreams do you remember?

3. Do you ever
   a. dream in color?
   b. dream in another language?
   c. dream about traveling to distant places?
   d. dream about people you know?
   e. find that your dreams come true?

4. Do you think that dreams have special meanings?

Support your answers by giving any examples or details that you can.

GETTING INFORMATION FROM ILLLUSTRATIONS

Look at the illustration and answer these questions.

1. How many REM cycles do we have?

2. What cycle lasts the longest?

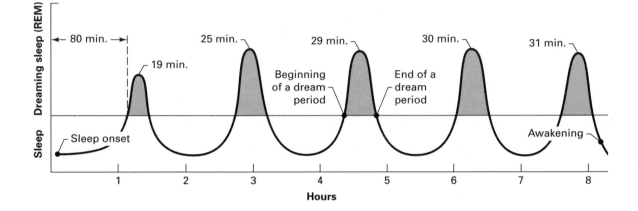

Understanding and Exploring Reading

PREVIEWING

Read the title and the first sentence of each paragraph in the reading. Based on that information, check (✓) the ideas you expect to find out about in this reading.

I expect to find out about

1. _____ the common ideas in dreams.

2. _____ the cycles and stages of dreaming.

3. _____ stories about the dreams people have.

4. _____ how dreaming changes as we get older.

Compare your choices with a partner. Try to agree on your answers. Then read all of the paragraphs. Check to see whether you should change any of the choices you made.

■■   *The Mystery of Dreams*   ■■

A. Do you remember your dreams? Do people have the same dreams? Why do we dream? There are many questions about dreams. We dream during the REM (rapid eye movement) stage of sleep. We have about five periods of REM sleep during the night. The first REM cycle lasts about 10 minutes. As the night goes on, the REM cycle gets longer. By early morning, the REM cycle can last up to 90 minutes. Usually, it is in this last REM cycle that we remember our dreams.

B. Dreams change as people age. Infants dream about half of the time they are asleep. But, of course, we don't know what it is they dream about. At age eight or nine, children start to tell their dreams as stories. People aged twenty-one to thirty-four report that many of their dreams are about feeling guilty for things that they did. Older men usually dream about work or their families.

C. Many dreams share common ideas and concerns. Some common dreams are about falling, flying, or floating in the sky. In many dreams, people forget something important, such as going to work on time or putting on clothes. In many dreams, people miss their bus, plane, or train, or they are late for an appointment. Most people's dreams have two other people in them. Bad dreams are more common than good ones. When people are in trouble, they often have negative dreams. People who are widowed or divorced dream about death more often than married people do. More women than men talk about their dreams.

D. Do you want to remember your dreams? If you wake up during a dream, you will remember it better. If you want to, you can train yourself to remember your dreams. One way is to tell yourself your dream when you wake. Keep a pen and paper or a tape recorder near your bed, and write or record what you dreamed about. When people are worried, they don't remember their dreams very well.

E. We never stop dreaming. But we can't really say what dreams mean or how they happen. Dreams are still a mystery.

UNDERSTANDING DETAILS

A. Circle *T* for true and *F* for false. In the reading, underline the words that provide support for your answers.

1. T F   We dream during the REM stage of sleep.

2. T F   We have only three periods of REM sleep during the night.

3. T F   As the night goes on, the REM cycles get shorter.

4. T F   Our dreams stay the same throughout our lives.

5. T F   Many people have dreams about ordinary things that could happen to them.

6. T F   Most people's dreams have other people in them.

7. T F   Good dreams are more common than bad dreams.

8. T F   A bad dream could be a sign of trouble in a person's life.

9. T F   Women report their dreams more often then men do.

10. T F   People can learn how to remember their dreams.

B. Answer the following questions.

1. How much of their sleep time do infants spend dreaming?

   _____

   _____

2. How do children tell about their dreams?

   _____

   _____

3. What kinds of dreams do people aged twenty-one to thirty-four have?

   _____

   _____

4. What do older men dream about?

   _____

   _____

5. What important things do people dream they forget to do?

   _____

   _____

6. What kinds of things do people dream they miss?

   _____

   _____

7. When will you better remember your dreams?

   _____

8. How can you remember your dreams?

   _____

   _____

9. When is it difficult for people to remember their dreams?

   _____

Work with a partner. Take turns reading the questions and answers. Refer to the reading if you have different answers.

After Reading

EVALUATING THE INFORMATION

Use the information from the reading to decide who is speaking. The choices include

a. a sleep expert.
b. the mother of an infant.
c. an eight-year-old child.
d. a twenty-four-year-old person.
e. an older man.

On the line after each statement, write the letter of the speaker. Give reasons to explain your choice, based on the reading.

1. I can't believe that she is dreaming. She's so young. What can she be dreaming about? But I can see that her eyes are moving back and forth. _____

2. I had a dream that I was talking with you and Harry. We were trying to finish the work on our project, but we couldn't find the last part of it. We looked everywhere without success. _____

3. I had a dream that I forgot your birthday present and didn't have anything to give you. I felt really bad, and I didn't know what I would say to you. _____

4. In my dream, there was a park. And we decided to play there. We took off our shoes to play in the sand. Then it started to rain, and I couldn't find my shoes. _____

5. Sleep research tells us that we dream during the REM stage of sleep. There are about five of these stages during a night of sleep. _____

Compare your answers with a partner. Take turns reading the statements and telling the identity of the speaker.

Vocabulary Building

VOCABULARY IN CONTEXT

A. Complete each statement with one of the nouns or verbs from the following list. Use the words in boldface to help you choose your answer.

a. appointment   b. change   c. divorced   d. dream

e. forget   f. remember   g. report   h. share   i. train

j. wake up   k. widowed   l. worried

1. They were _____ **after five years of marriage, because they were unhappy**.

2. You have to _____ at 7:00 if you want **to get to school on time**.

3. I wanted to _____ what she said **because it was important**.

4. When people are _____, they **don't sleep very well**.

5. Last night, I had a strange _____ **about my grandparents**.

6. **As people get older**, they _____ in many different ways.

7. I have an _____ to see **him at 9:00, and I don't want to be late**.

8. I never _____ my dreams, because **I tell myself to remember** before I go to sleep.

9. She was _____, and it was difficult for her to enjoy **life without her husband**.

10. I have **to travel** by _____ if I want to visit her.

11. She asked everyone to _____what he or she saw **so that everyone would know what happened**.

12. **We are similar** in that we _____ a love for languages.

Expanding Your Language

SPEAKING

Discussion Questions: People all over the world dream. Do different cultures see dreams and dreaming differently? Get together in a small group with people from different counties, from different parts of the world. Find out from one another the following things:

1. What different kinds of dreams do people have?

2. What are the meanings of dreams?

3. What stories or myths are there about dreams and their meanings?

4. What are some examples of happy dreams, scary dreams, dreams that tell the future, and dreams that return more than once?

WRITING

Topic Writing: From the ideas in the chapter and your own experience, write ten to fifteen sentences about the topic of dreams. To do this, follow these steps:

1. Use the following outline to help yourself make a few notes before you begin to write.

   ▪ **Write some facts about when people dream.**

   The sleep cycle

      a. REM _____

      b. _____

   How long does each cycle last?

      First: _____

      Second: _____

      Third: _____

      Fourth: _____

      Fifth: _____

   How does it change as people get older?

   ▪ **Write some facts about the types of dreams people have.**

      No. 1: _____

      No. 2: _____

      No. 3: _____

   ▪ **Write some facts about how to remember dreams.**

      No. 1: _____

      No. 2: _____

      No. 3: _____

2. Work with a partner. Use your outline to help you tell your partner what you plan to write about. Listen to your partner's outline of ideas. Compare the two outlines. Make any changes you need to improve your outline.

3. Write as much as you can. Write in complete sentences. Use your notes to help you write.

Read On: Taking It Further

READING CLOZE

Use the words listed here from the unit to fill in the blanks in this paragraph.

a. asleep (2×)   b. awake (2×)   c. breathing   d. dreaming

e. enough   f. feels   g. hours   h. longer   i. need

j. remember   k. sleep (2×)

What happens when we (1) _____? When we fall

(2) _____, our brain and body activity decreases. Our

heart-beats and (3) _____ get slower. Our brain waves get

slower and (4) _____ or deeper. This sleep takes place

during the first (5) _____ after we fall

(6) _____. As we continue to sleep, our brains send out

small, fast waves similar to when we are (7)_____. Our
eyes are moving under the eyelids. This shows that we are

(8) _____.

   We usually (9) _____ the last dream of the

night. Normally, people (10) _____ 7–10 hours of

(11) _____ each night. But many of us are not getting

(12) _____ sleep. Without sleep, a person

(13) _____ tired and has difficulty thinking and staying

(14) _____. But getting a good night's sleep solves these
problems.

Check your answers.

READING SUGGESTIONS

■ *READING TIP:* Don't forget to write in your notebook your reading journal and vocabulary log entries. Show your entry logs to your teacher.

Ask your teacher to suggest a story or an article to read on the topic of sleep and dreams.

    Sample suggestion: Dreamcatchers are common in North American Indian culture. They are objects that look like a spider's web. They are hung near where a person sleeps. They are meant to catch bad dreams before they can enter a person's mind. Read about dreamcatchers or other dream customs from different cultures.

WORD PLAY: A SPELLING GAME

You can use vocabulary from the chapter readings to play this game. Think of a pair of words, such as *dream* and *mystery*. The last letter of *dream* (m) is the first letter of *mystery*. Select a partner and follow these rules to play the game.

1. From the reading, make a list of seven to ten words that can be paired with another word.

2. Give your partner the first word to spell.

3. Your partner spells the word and then must select a new word that begins with the last letter of the word spelled (time limit: 1 minute). You must spell this word. If your partner can't find a word, you supply an answer, and your partner continues to spell.

4. Continue to take turns until the teacher calls time (after about 10 minutes).

5. The pair that correctly chooses and spells the most words wins.

Relationships

Every community has its own customs and traditions.

—Philippine Proverb

Introducing the Topics

We meet people every day. People have many different kinds of relationships with one another. These relationships can be easy or difficult, long or short. As we make contact with various people, our lives change. This unit touches on some of the types of relationships people enjoy. Chapter 7 looks at some dating customs now and in the past. In Chapter 8, you'll read about the stories of two unusual weddings. Chapter 9 focuses on the ways neighbors are meeting to help one another out.

Points of Interest

What kind of relationship do you think these people have?

CHAPTER 7

Is Dating Still the Same?

Chapter Openers

DISCUSSION QUESTIONS: DATING CUSTOMS

Think about these questions. Share your ideas with a partner or in a small group.

1. What is a date? What does it mean to go on a date?

2. Why do people go on dates? Do or did you ever go on dates?

3. Where are some good places to go and good things to do on a date?

4. How much money do you usually spend on a date?

5. Who usually asks for a date: the man, the woman, or either?

6. How is dating today different from dating in the past

    a   in the United States?

    b. in other countries?

Exploring and Understanding Reading

PREDICTING

This is an interview with a twenty-year-old man and a fifty-five year-old woman about the way dating today is different from the way it was in the past. What questions do you think that Dave, the interviewer, will ask? Write three questions.

1. _____

2. _____

3. _____

With a partner, compare your questions. Then quickly read the interview. Check any of the predicted questions you find.

■■ _____

Dating: What's Changed and What Hasn't

David: They say that in the 1970s, you could meet people to date at bars; in the 1980s, at health clubs; and in the 1990s, at bookstores. I want to find out about the differences between dating now and the way it was in the 1960s. Susan Harding, fifty-five, and Jerry Brown, twenty, are here with me today. Let me ask you both this question: Where would you go to meet people you'd like to date?

Susan: Well, I didn't start to date until I was sixteen. In my day, there were lots of places to go and meet someone interesting. I went to school dances, ballgames, church activities, and summer camp; that was the best.

Jerry: Well, it's not as easy to meet people today. Sometimes, I meet people at work or at the gym. I know one person who met someone through a personal ad in the newspaper. Some people go to bars or clubs to meet people, but that's not for me. Then there's the Internet. But I think that it's unusual to actually get to know someone through the Internet.

Susan: We didn't have the Internet, but we did have blind dates. A friend would arrange for you to go out with someone you didn't know at all—a stranger. Sometimes, it worked. My brother met his wife on a blind date.

David: Suppose you meet someone you like. Who does the asking: the man or the woman?

Susan: In my day, the man always asked the woman out.

Jerry: That's not true today. Both men and women ask each other out. It doesn't matter.

David: What about clothes? Would you wear something special or get something new to wear?

Jerry: I would. Clothes are expensive, but I like to wear things that make me look good.

Susan: I never spent a lot of time and money on clothes. That was only when I had a special date, such as a formal dance or the senior prom.

David: Who pays for the date?

Jerry: It depends. If I ask someone out, I usually pay. If she asks me out, we split the bill.

Susan: Well, usually the man paid. But sometimes we'd "go Dutch"; I paid for my bill, and he'd pay for his.

Dave: How much would it cost to go out on a typical date?

Susan: In 1960, movie tickets for two people cost about $2.00. Dinner, including wine, for two in a good restaurant cost about $10.00. A dozen roses cost about $5.00. In all, it was about one day's pay.

Jerry: Today, it can cost $100–$130 for movie tickets, dinner, and flowers. It's about half a week's pay. But, actually, my idea of a special date is to go somewhere that doesn't cost a lot of money—somewhere where you can relax and get to know each other. In my neighborhood, there's a bookstore/café that's the best.

Susan: I agree. My best dates were going to this little coffeeshop and sitting for hours, talking.

UNDERSTANDING DETAILS

A. Circle *T* if the statement is true and *F* is the statement is false. In the reading, underline the words that support your answer. Correct any information that is false.

1. T F Today, it is more difficult to meet people you'd like to date.

2. T F You could meet someone you liked on a blind date.

3. T F In the past, women asked men out on dates.

4. T F Susan and Jerry both spend time and money on getting the right clothes.

5. T F In the past, men usually paid for the cost of a date.

6. T F Today, dates are more expensive than in the past.

7. T F Susan and Jerry both like dates that don't cost a lot of money.

B. Answer the following questions. In the reading, circle the parts that support your answer. Write the question number in the margin.

1. Where did Susan go to meet people she could date?

   _____

   _____

2. Where does Jerry meet people he could date?

   _____

   _____

3. When did Susan spend money on clothes for a date?

   _____

   _____

4. Does Jerry spend money on clothes for a date? Explain.

   _____

   _____

5. Does Jerry usually pay for a date? Explain.

   _____

   _____

6. How does the cost of Susan's date in 1960 compare to the cost of Jerry's date today?

   _____

   _____

7. What is their idea of a special date?

   _____

   _____

Work with a partner. Read your questions and answers. Refer to the reading if you have different answers.

C. Identifying the Speaker: Who said that? Write the name of the person who said the following questions or statements.

1. _____ The man asked the woman out.

2. _____ How much would it cost to go out on a date?

3. _____ A dozen roses cost about $5.00.

4. _____ A friend would arrange for you to go out with someone you didn't know at all.

5. _____ Clothes are expensive, but I like to wear clothes that make me look good.

6. _____ Usually, I pay for the date if I ask someone out.

7. _____ Where would you go to meet people you'd like to date?

8. _____ My idea of a special date is to go somewhere that doesn't cost a lot of money.

Check your answers. Work with a partner. Take turns reading the statements.

After Reading

EVALUATING THE INFORMATION: CATEGORIZING

What do Susan and Jerry say? Complete the chart, based on the information you read.

Idea	Susan	Jerry
1. Where to meet people to date:		
2. Who pays for the date:		
3. What does it cost:		
4. Suggestion for a special date:		

With a partner, compare your charts.

DISCUSSION QUESTIONS: AGREE/DISAGREE

Based on the information in this chapter and your own experience, circle *A* if you agree or *D* if you disagree with these statements. Work with a partner or others in a small group to share your ideas. Give the reasons for your answers.

1. A D   Sixteen is a good age to begin dating.

2. A D   Going on a date is a good way to get to know someone.

3. A D   Dating is too expensive.

4. A D   Parents should know whom you are dating.

5. A D   In the future, dating will disappear.

GETTING INFORMATION FROM ILLUSTRATIONS

Based on the information from the reading, write the time period for each of these photos.

1960s   1970s   1980s   1990s

1. _____   2. _____   3. _____   4. _____

Work with a partner. Give reasons for your choices. Together, write your own captions for these photos.

Vocabulary Building

VOCABULARY IN CONTEXT

Complete each sentence with one of the words from the following list. Use the words in boldface to help you choose your answer.

a. arrange   b. cost   c. dated   d. differences   e. meet

f. split   g. stranger   h. unusual

1. Let's _____ the bill; **you pay half and I'll pay half.**

2. At first, I thought he was a _____, **but then I remembered his name and where we'd met before.**

3. **How much** does the ticket _____?

4. I met **a girl my brother liked** and _____ a few times when he was in high school.

5. Could you _____ for me to be introduced to your brother **before the party begins**?

6. There are so many _____ between them; they have **nothing in common**.

7. Hello, it's so nice to finally _____ you after **hearing so much about you**.

8. It's so _____ to find **anyone who likes this kind of music**.

WORD FORMS: VERBS

A. Write the past form of the following verbs. Circle the forms of these verbs that you find in the reading.

Present Tense   *Past Tense*

1. do   _____

2. meet   _____

3. date   _____

4. have   _____

5. work   _____

6. pay   _____

7. cost   _____

8. is   _____

B. Write two sentences and two questions of your own, using the present and past tenses of the verbs in both the affirmative and negative forms of the verbs.

Affirmative

1. _____

2. _____

Negative

1. _____

2. _____

Questions

1. _____

2. _____

Expanding Your Language

SPEAKING

Role Play—Interviewing: Prepare an interview like the one you read in this chapter. You can choose the same topic or one that is similar, such as marriage. Work with a partner or in a small group. Decide on the roles you will act out. Include the role of the interviewer. Prepare a list of questions for the interviewer to ask. Prepare the answers that your characters will give. Write out the script for the interview. Use your script to act out the interview, but do not memorize the lines. Be creative.

WRITING

Interview: Talk to three people about a date they have gone on. Complete the following chart to prepare notes to write from.

	Where did you go?	*What did you do?*	*Was it interesting or not?*	*Explain.*
Name 1:				
Name 2:				
Name 3:				

Use your notes to write about dating. You can include information comparing dating now to dating in the past or about dating in different countries. Write about an interesting date that you had or would like to go on.

CHAPTER 8

A Different Kind of Wedding

Chapter Openers

DISCUSSION QUESTIONS: GETTING MARRIED

Think about these questions. Share your ideas with a partner or in a small group.

1. At what age do people usually get married?

2. What happens at wedding ceremonies you know of; what do people do and say?

3. Why do people decide to get married; why not?

4. Compare wedding ceremonies today and in the past; how are they the same, and how are they different?

5. What kind of wedding ceremony did you or would you like to have?

PAIRED READINGS

These are two reports of very unusual weddings. Read and find out why. Choose one of the reports to read. Work with a partner who is reading the same report.

■ ■

Reading 1: Janet's Unusual Wedding

PREDICTING: GETTING INFORMATION FROM ILLUSTRATIONS

Work with your partner and take turns explaining what you see in the picture. Answer the following question.

What could be unusual about Janet's wedding?

Exploring and Understanding Reading

UNDERSTANDING THE MAIN IDEA

Read the story. Then check your prediction. Correct it, if necessary. What is the main idea of this story?

UNDERSTANDING DETAILS

Answer the questions after each paragraph. In the story, underline the facts that support your answer. Write the question number in the margin of the reading.

The Woman Who Married Herself

A.   Janet Downes is planning a traditional wedding. She has a wedding gown, a choir to sing wedding songs, flowers, and a cake. But there is one difference. It's not a legal wedding. On June 27, Janet is planning to marry *herself*. Janet decided to marry herself on her fortieth birthday.

———————————

1. What is Janet planning to have at her wedding?

———————————————————————————

———————————————————————————

2. What is different about Janet's wedding?

———————————————————————————

———————————————————————————

3. When is Janet planning to get married?

———————————————————————————

———————————————————————————

4. Why did she choose this day?

———————————————————————————

B.   The wedding is a celebration to say that she is happy with her life. She bought a ring to wear. She will say "I, Janet Downes, take myself with all of my strengths and faults to be my lawfully wedded wife…." The choir will sing some special songs. They include the song "My Way" by Frank Sinatra.

———————————

1. Why is she having this wedding?

———————————————————————————

———————————————————————————

2. What did she buy to wear?

_____

_____

3. What songs will the choir sing?

_____

_____

C. Janet is inviting 200 friends and relatives to this special wedding. One guest is her fiancé. They have been together for 4 years. Will they get legally married? Janet is thinking about it. She thinks that they will get married in the future. But for now, she is happy to be marrying herself.

_____

1. How many people is Janet inviting to the wedding?

_____

_____

2. Who is one guest who will be there?

_____

_____

3. What are Janet's future plans?

_____

_____

4. How is she feeling now?

_____

_____

Work with a partner. Take turns reading the questions and answers. Refer to the reading if your answers are different.

RECAPPING THE STORY

Reread the first paragraph quickly. Cover the information and tell your partner as much as you can remember. Ask for help if you forget or give incorrect information. Ask your partner to retell the information. Take turns reading and retelling the information in all of the paragraphs.

REACTING TO THE STORY

Discuss these questions with your partner.

1. What do you think of Janet's wedding? Explain whether you agree or disagree with what she did. Give the reasons for your opinion.

2. What would you say to Janet if you were
   a. her mother or father?
   b. her fiancé?
   c. her friend?

Reading 2: Dave's Unusual Wedding

PREDICTING: GETTING INFORMATION FROM ILLUSTRATIONS AND TITLES

Work with your partner and take turns explaining what you see in the picture. Read the story title on the following page. Answer the following questions.

What is unusual about Dave's plan?

_____

Exploring and Understanding Reading

UNDERSTANDING THE MAIN IDEA

Read the story. Then check your prediction. Correct it, if necessary. What is the main idea of this story?

_____

UNDERSTANDING DETAILS

Answer the questions after each paragraph. In the story, underline the facts that support your answer. Write the question number in the margin of the reading.

The Man Who Advertised for a Bride

A.   Dave Weinlick is a graduate student in anthropology. He is an independent, creative person, and he is preparing for his wedding. He has a tuxedo, the rings, a minister, and musicians. He has a place for the reception after the ceremony. One thing is missing: a bride. He will meet the bride the day of his wedding. Dave is advertising for a bride. He put an ad in the newspaper and on the Internet.

_____

1. Who is Dave Weinlick?

_____

_____

2. What kind of person is he?

_____

_____

3. What does he have for his wedding?

_____

_____

4. Why is Dave advertising?

_____

_____

5. Where is he advertising?

_____

_____

B.   In the ad, Dave asks women to come to a special reception before the wedding ceremony. Women can bring their friends and families. Dave and his friends will interview the brides-to-be. The women and their friends and families will interview Dave. Everyone will take a vote, and Dave will marry the winner.

_____

1. Where does Dave ask women to come?

_____

_____

2. Whom can the women bring?

_____

_____

3. What will Dave and his friends do?

_____

_____

4. What will the women and their friends and families do?

_____

_____

5. Whom will Dave marry?

_____

_____

C.   Dave says that his plan is unusual but that he really wants to get married. He is looking for "the right woman." Dave's father, Herman, is not happy about his son's plan. Herman says, "I admire his independence in many things, but not this. I think he should take marriage more seriously." Matt Gundlich is a marriage counselor. He doesn't think that Dave's plan will work. He doesn't think that your friends can choose a good partner for you. Only you can choose the person you marry.

_____

1. How does Dave feel about getting married?

    _____

    _____

2. Whom is Dave looking for?

    _____

    _____

3. How does Dave's father feel about the plan? Explain.

    _____

    _____

4. Who is Matt Gundlich?

    _____

    _____

5. What does he think of Dave's plan?

    _____

    _____

6. What does Matt think is the problem with Dave's plan?

    _____

    _____

Work with a partner. Take turns reading the questions and answers. Refer to the reading if you have different answers.

RECAPPING THE STORY

Reread the first paragraph quickly. Then cover the information and tell your partner as much as you can remember. Ask for help if you forget or give incorrect information. Ask your partner to retell the information. Take turns reading and retelling the information in all of the paragraphs.

REACTING TO THE STORY

Discuss these questions with your partner.

1. What do you think of Dave's wedding plan? Would you agree or disagree with him. Give reasons for your opinion.

2. What would you say to Dave if you were
   a. his mother or father?
   b. his fiancée?
   c. his fiancée's family?
   d. his friend?
   e. her friend?

After Reading

COMPARING THE STORIES

Work with a partner who read a different story. Together, complete the following chart.

Questions	Janet	Dave
1. What kind of people are they? (Give a description)		
2. Where will they get married?		
3. What will they have at the wedding?		
4. Who will come to the wedding?		
5. Whom are they marrying?		
6. How did they find their fiancé(e)s?		
7. How long have they known their fiancé(e)s?		
8. What do their families and friends think of their plans?		

From the information in the chart, circle the things that the people in these stories share in common. Prepare to explain what is similar in the two stories.

REACTING TO THE STORY

Discuss the questions in the section "Reacting to the Story" for both readings. In addition, decide what you think about the following questions.

1. Do you think that Janet will marry her fiancé in the future? Why or why not?

2. Do you think that Dave's marriage plans will be successful? Why or why not?

3. What questions would you ask Dave or Janet about their plans?

4. What are the different ways that people choose someone to marry? In your opinion, what are the best ways?

5. Is it more difficult to find a person to marry now than in the past? Give reasons for your answers.

■ Vocabulary Building

VOCABULARY IN CONTEXT

Complete each sentence with one of the words from the following list. Use the words in boldface to help you choose your answer.

a. advertising   b. choose   c include   d. interview

e. marry   f. reception   g. traditional

1. The ceremony will _____ a special song **and other pieces** sung by the choir.

2. He will _____ the bride and her family and, **after talking with them**, make his choice.

3. She will _____ on June 27 and **celebrate her wedding** at a party that evening.

4. It's **not always easy to make up your mind** and

   _____ the person who will be right for you.

5. After the wedding takes place, she will **meet her guests** at a

   _____ at her parents' house.

6. He is _____ for a bride **in the newspaper and on the Internet**.

7. She is planning to have a _____ wedding **similar to many of the weddings in her family**.

Check your answers. Take turns reading your sentences.

MATCHING MEANINGS: ANTONYMS

Match the word in Column A with its opposite in Column B.

Column A   **Column B**

_____ 1. future   a. unusual

_____ 2. dependent   b. together

_____ 3. difference   c. independent

_____ 4. nontraditional   d. wife

_____ 5. ordinary   e. past

_____ 6. usual   f. traditional

_____ 7. apart   g. similarity

_____ 8. husband   h. special

Check your answers. Write three sentences with words from these lists. Use two words from the lists in each sentence.

1. _____

2. _____

3. _____

CATEGORIZING

In each of these groups, circle the word that does not belong. Prepare to explain the reason for your choice.

1. reception   ceremony   strength   wedding   celebration

2. independent   creative   special   happy   counselor

3. friend   unusual   family   father   fiancé

4. think   decide   plan   choose   sing

5. ring   apartment   gown   flowers   tuxedo

Pair Work: Tell your answer and the reason it doesn't belong.

Expanding Your Language

SPEAKING

A. Role Play: Work with a partner. Choose the role of one of the people in these stories, such as Dave and his father or Janet and her fiancé. Together, write out the conversation between these two people, based on the story and on ideas of your own.

Here is one example of how to begin the conversation:

Dave: Good news, Dad. I've decided to get married.
Father: Married? What do you mean? To whom?

B. Two-Minute Taped Talk: Record a 2-minute audiotape about one of the stories in this chapter. To make your tape, follow the steps on page 60.

WRITING

A. Writing Sentences from Information in a Graph: Look at the following graph and use the information to write sentences of your own about married or single Americans.

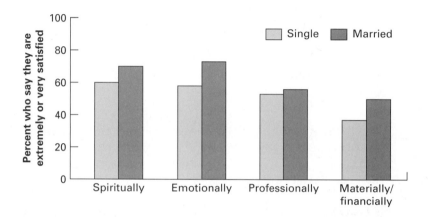

Example: Fifty percent of *married* Americans say that they are very satisfied with their lives financially. Thirty-seven percent of *single* Americans say that they are very satisfied with their lives financially. Thirteen percent more *married* Americans are very satisfied with their lives financially than are *single* Americans.

1. _____

   _____

   _____

   _____

2. _____

   _____

   _____

   _____

B. Personal Writing: Based on the ideas you discussed in this chapter, as well as any ideas of your own, write ten to fifteen sentences about one of the following:

1. The kind of wedding that you had or would have in the future.

2. The life of a single person compared to the life of a married person.

CHAPTER 9

Neighbors

Chapter Openers

MATCHING MEANINGS

A. Match the word in Column A with the definition of that word in Column B.

Column A

_____ 1. neighbors

_____ 2. neighborhood

Column B

a. An area where people live and that has its own special identity

b. People who live near or next to one another

Work with a partner to discuss your answers.

B. Think of some examples of neighborhoods that you have lived in or have heard about. Describe what they are like.

AGREE/DISAGREE

Read the following statements. Write _A_ if you agree or _D_ if you disagree. Give the reasons for your choices.

_____ 1. People who live in the neighborhood usually know one another.

_____ 2. You can call a neighbor for help if you are feeling sick or need to go to the hospital.

_____ 3. Neighbors don't talk to one another very often.

_____ 4. You can call your neighbor to help if you have problems with your heat, water, or electricity.

_____ 5. Neighbors get together for fun activities, such as street parties or barbecues.

_____ 6. People can ask their neighbors when they need to borrow ordinary things, such as chairs and tables, or food, such as sugar or milk.

_____ 7. Neighbors often help one another to look after their children.

Discuss your answers with others in a small group.

Exploring and Understanding Reading

PREVIEWING

■ *READING TIP:*
Remember that previewing is an important critical-reading skill. Using this technique helps you to find some of the important ideas in a reading. Then it will be easier to understand the rest of the information and to guess at the meaning of new vocabulary when you read the whole selection.

To preview, read the title and the first and last sentences of each paragraph in the reading. Based on that information, check (✔) the ideas you expect to find out about from the following list.

I expect to find out about:

1. _____ the stories of people who are good neighbors.

2. _____ how to make your neighborhood safe from crime.

3. _____ different ways neighbors help one another.

4. _____ the difficulties of meeting your neighbors.

5. _____ the reasons people get to know their neighbors.

6. _____ stories of people who fall in love with their neighbors.

Compare your choices with a partner. Try to agree on your answers. Then read all of the paragraphs. See whether you should change any of the choices you made.

In the Neighborhood: Modern Success Stories

A. In this neighborhood, there are a number of people who are in need of a little help. Cynthia Marks is a single mother who finds it difficult to work at her office all day and to put dinner on the table every night for her four kids. "Usually, I'm so tired at the end of the day that I bring home pizza for them to eat." Cynthia decided that she had to do something. She didn't want to spend her food budget on expensive take-out food. Also, she wanted her kids to have a well-balanced, nutritious meal. She talked to her neighbor, Ann Cullen, another single mother with two children, who works full time as a lawyer. Ann understood Cynthia's needs. She too often felt impatient and angry having to cook and clean after working all day. She didn't want to be angry, and she wanted to

spend more time with her kids at home. So the two neighbors thought of a plan. They decided that they would take turns cooking for each other's families once a week.

B. There are hundreds of neighborhoods in which people need some help to do ordinary chores. Neighborhood groups exist to help people in a number of different ways. There are groups that take older people who can no longer drive or take public transportation to do their grocery shopping on their own. There are neighborhood crime-watch groups that keep an eye on people's homes and watch for any signs of robberies or other crimes. There are child-safety programs that ask adults to watch out for neighborhood children who may need to come to a safe home in an emergency.

C. Cynthia and Ann's plan was a success. They now share meal making and sometimes eat together with three other neighbors. According to Ann, cooking for a group once a week is better than cooking five nights a week for three. In addition to sharing dinner, Cynthia and Ann get to talk about their problems and responsibilities. With their neighbors, they discuss the neighborhood school their young children attend and let each other know about special sales in neighborhood stores or social events that will be taking place. According to these women, they have a relationship that has improved their lives.

NOTE TAKING: FINDING THE KEY WORDS

A. Answer these questions in notes. When you write notes, remember to write only the key words, not the whole sentence. In the story, underline the key words and write the question numbers in the margin near the line where you found the information.

> ▪ *NOTE-TAKING TIP:*
> *Key words are the words that are important to understanding the ideas. Look at the key words in boldface in this sentence: She **brought** the **children** their **dinner**. Usually, the nouns and verbs in a sentence are key words. Questions after a reading help you find the key words you need to underline.*

1. What is some personal information about Cynthia and Ann?

	Cynthia	*Ann*
a. Marital status:		
b. Employment:		
c. Children:		

2. What problems do Cynthia and Ann have?

	Cynthia	*Ann*
a. Problem:		
b. Feelings:		
c. Didn't want:		
d. Wanted:		
e. Solution:		

3. According to the reading, what are some ways that neighborhood groups can help people?

People and Problems	*Help that Some People Can Offer*
a.	
b.	
c.	

4. What do Cynthia, Ann, and their neighbors talk about when they meet for dinner?

a. _____

b. _____

Work with a partner. Take turns answering the questions. Refer to the story if you have different information.

B. Circle *T* for true and *F* for false. Use the information from your notes if you are not sure of the answer.

1. T F Cynthia and Ann are both single mothers.

2. T F Cynthia and Ann both have four children.

3. T F Cynthia feels angry and impatient at night.

4. T F Cynthia and Ann decided to take turns cooking for each other's families twice a week.

5. T F There are a number of neighborhood groups that help others.

6. T F Older people can always drive or take public transportation to do their shopping.

7. T F Crime-watch groups watch their neighbors' homes.

8. T F There are no safe homes for children in the neighborhood.

9. T F Cynthia and Ann now cook for a group of people every night.

10. T F Cynthia and Ann like to talk about their work problems at dinner.

Work with a partner. Take turns answering the questions. Refer to the reading in cases where you disagree.

After Reading

REACTING TO THE READING

Discuss these questions with a partner or others in a small group.

1. What do Cynthia and Ann enjoy about being neighbors?

2. When do neighbors get to meet one another in your neighbor-hood; for example, would you meet your neighbors at church, at the store, at the gym, or at a meeting?

3. Is it more difficult for neighbors to get to know one another in other countries than in the United States? Why or why not?

4. What is your neighborhood like? Describe the people and places that you know.

5. What makes a neighborhood attractive or interesting to people? What makes it uninteresting or unattractive to people?

6. Do you enjoy cooking or eating in a group? Why or why not?

Vocabulary Building

VOCABULARY IN CONTEXT

A. Complete each sentence with one of the words from the fol-lowing list. Decide whether you need a noun, an adjective, or a verb in the sentence. Look for clues in the sentence to help you understand the meaning. In the sentence, underline the words that helped you to choose your answer.

a. attend   b. chores   c. discuss   d. ordinary

e. responsibilities   f. spend

1. The neighborhood looks very _____, but the relation-ships that people have there are very special.

2. She has so many different _____ that she doesn't have enough time to relax.

3. They felt very tired and didn't want to finish the household

   _____, such as the laundry and the shopping.

4. How much time to you need to _____ on making dinner?

5. Did you _____ the meeting last week? I don't remember seeing you.

6. I need to _____ this problem with you. When can we meet to talk?

Check your answers. Work with a partner. Take turns reading the statements.

B. Circle *N* if the word in boldface is a noun, or *V* if it is a verb. Then write a sentence using the word as a different part of speech.

1. N   V   She has a lot of different **needs** that are difficult to meet.

2. N   V   Her **work** is very important to her.

3. N   V   Can I **help** you to carry in those packages?

4. N   V   She decided to **share** her sandwich with him because she wasn't very hungry.

5. N   V   Can you **budget** enough money for us to pay for new equipment?

6. N   V   Will the disk **drive** work on this computer?

7. N   V   If they **sign** the card today, we can send it in the mail.

Check your answers.

PREPOSITIONS

Complete these sentences with the correct preposition from the following list.

a. in   b. for   c. of   d. with   e. to   f. on

1. They decided to try cooking ———— each other.

2. She helped him in a number ———— different ways.

3. She lived ———— this neighborhood ———— many years.

4. They worked together ———— three other women.

5. According ———— the experts, this program will help you.

6. Your neighbors will keep an eye ———— your house during the day.

In the reading, find three sentences with prepositions. Circle the preposition and the word or words that go with it. Check your answers. Take turns reading the sentences.

Expanding Your Language

SPEAKING

Talk It Out: Think about the topic of neighbors. Make a list of the benefits of knowing your neighbors and then a list of the problems with neighbors. Look at the sample ideas and add three ideas of your own.

Benefits of Knowing Your Neighbors

- I can call if I need a ride to school.

- I can borrow milk if I run out of it at night.

- ————————————————

- ————————————————

- ————————————————

Problems with Neighbors

Loud music bothers me at night.

They often argue with me.

————————————————

————————————————

————————————————

Work with a partner and compare your lists. Discuss your own experiences with neighbors.

WRITING

A. Personal Reactions: Look closely at the neighborhood you live in now. Compare that neighborhood to another neighborhood, such as the one where you grew up. Write about both places, and compare the people and places of both neighborhoods. Work with a partner and describe the neighborhoods you wrote about.

B. What is your idea of an ideal neighborhood? What would it look like? In the space below, draw what it would look like.

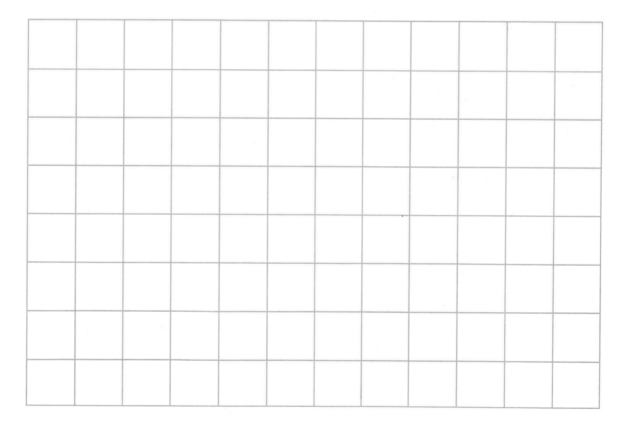

C. Use your drawing to explain your ideal neighborhood to another student.

Read On: Taking It Further

READING CLOZE

Use words from the unit as listed here to fill in the blanks in this paragraph.

a. date (2×)   b. describe (2×)   c. find   d. give

e. have   f. meet   g. number   h. old   i. popular

j. put   k. tall

How do people meet others they would like to date? One way is to

(1) _____ an ad in the personals section of the newspa-

per. Advertising for a (2)_____ is not a new idea; it is

almost as (3)_____ as newspapers are. Putting an adver-

tisement in the personals is still (4)_____ today. But
many people say that this is not the way to find a date. What are the

problems? One man said that his (5) _____ didn't look

like the description she gave. She didn't (6)_____ blond

hair and wasn't (7)_____ and thin. Another problem is

that it's difficult to (8)_____ yourself in an ad. Most ads

are about 100 words. It's difficult to (9)_____ yourself in

100 words. But even if you don't (10) _____ anyone
interesting, personals give you a chance to introduce yourself to
someone new. But remember this advice: Be sure to

(11)_____ in a public place, such as a coffee shop or a

bar. And never (12) _____ your home address or phone

(13)_____.

Check your answers.

NEWSPAPER ARTICLES

■ *READING TIP:* Don't forget to write your reading journal and vocabulary log entries in your notebook.

Check the newspaper for articles about marriages or other relationships you read about in this unit. Ask your teacher for short articles that you can read. One suggestion is to look for articles about relationships in an advice column in the newspaper. Read the article over until you have a good idea of the important facts of the story. Explain your article to a partner or in a small group.

The Challenge of Sports Today

The first thing is to love your sport. Never do it to please someone else. It has to be yours.

– Peggy Fleming

Introducing the Topics

Sports today are both very difficult and very exciting. In this unit, you will find out about a variety of sports that appeal to various types of people. Chapter 10 is about competing in a new sport, the triathlon, and the development of this recent sport. Chapter 11 compares the thrills of outdoor and indoor sports events. Chapter 12 takes a look at the types of preparations today's Olympic athletes make.

Points of Interest

What kinds of challenges do you think this person faced?

CHAPTER 10

The Challenge of the Triathlon

Chapter Openers

GETTING INFORMATION FROM ILLUSTRATIONS

A. On the line under each picture, write the letter of the statement that it best matches.

_____   _____   _____   _____

a. Triathletes are very dedicated people. They spend hours training before a competition.

b. After they finish swimming, triathletes compete in a long bicycle race.

c. Triathletes finish the event with a marathon distance run.

d. The triathlon begins with a swimming race.

B. Describe what people do in the triathlon: what they need in order to compete, where they train and compete, and why they like the triathlon event. Give your opinion of the triathlon: Is it difficult or not?

DISCUSSION QUESTIONS: PRACTICING SPORTS

Think about these questions. Discuss your ideas with a partner or in a small group.

1. What are some sports you like to practice? Give the reasons you like the sport.

2. What are some sports you like to watch?

3. What is enjoyable or difficult about each of these sports:
   a. bicycling
   b. swimming
   c. running

4. What do athletes have to do to prepare for sports competitions? What is the reason that people devote time to prepare for competitions?

■ Understanding and Exploring Reading

PREDICTING

Circle *T* for true or *F* for false.

1. T F   The triathlon has three events in one competition.

2. T F   It takes 24 hours to complete a triathlon.

3. T F   It takes many years of training to prepare for a triathlon race.

4. T F   The triathlon is a very old sports event.

5. T F   Only top athletes in their twenties compete in triathlons.

6. T F   The triathlon is an Olympic sport.

Quickly read the following selection. Check your answers after you finish the reading. Make any changes necessary.

■ ■

Getting Ready for the "Ironman"

■ *READING TIP: To read quickly, look at groups of two or three words together. Don't read one word at a time. Continue reading through the information until you reach the end. Then return to the start of the article to reread.*

A.   The triathlon is a demanding sport. Many say that it is a real test of an athlete's body and mind. It is difficult because it is three sports in one. It includes swimming for 2.4 miles (3.84 kilometers), bicycling for 112 miles (180 kilometers), and running for 26.2 miles (41.9 kilometers). It takes a lot of strength and willpower to compete. The top triathletes finish all three events in about 8 hours. This sport is a real challenge. First, it takes time and stamina to train for competitions. Some people spend up to 8 months training for the race. The training demands a lot of physical energy and strength. During training, the athletes will bike 320 km, swim 10 km, and run 56 km every week. Second, it takes money to compete. The equipment is not cheap. Bicycles for this event can cost up to $10,000. Top-quality swimming gear and running shoes are expensive. Athletes have to pay to enter the race. Third, athletes must have strong minds. It takes willpower to push themselves to keep training to reach their goal.

B.   The triathlon is a recent sport. Triathlons began in California in the early 1970s. There, some athletes started the three-sport race because they wanted to make their training exciting. One of these athletes moved to Hawaii and took the sport with him. In 1978, competitors held the first professional triathlon race in Hawaii. It was called the Ironman World Championship. In 1982, this race became famous because of the televised performance of Julie Moss. She was twenty-three years old, and it was her first competition. Exhausted, she was running toward the finish line. Suddenly, 3 meters before the line, she fell down. She tried to get up, but she kept falling. She finally crawled across the finish line. Television cameras showed the world her dramatic struggle. She lost that year, but she tried again. Finally, in 1985, she won Ironman Japan. This was the start of the Ironman's popularity.

C.   Today, triathlons are much more popular among ordinary athletes. People of all ages—from teens to seventies—can compete, as long as they are in good physical condition. In fact, it has become a great family sport, with fathers and mothers training with their sons and daughters. Triathletes are special people who have time in their lives for careers and families. Most are highly educated and earn top salaries in their jobs. They are people who are very competitive. Many triathletes are happily married. In fact, two-thirds of triathletes say that their training has a positive influence on their marriages. Today, the triathlon is an Olympic sport and a respected event worldwide.

UNDERSTANDING THE MAIN IDEAS

Write the letter of the paragraph that best fits each of these main ideas.

1. _____ Today, the triathlon is a sport that many people can train to compete in.

2. _____ Triathlon competitions are a new development in the history of sport.

3. _____ A triathlete has to be very strong in many different ways to practice this sport.

UNDERSTANDING DETAILS

A. Complete the following statements. In the margin of the reading where you found the information, write the question numbers.

1. The triathlon is a test of an athlete's
   a. mind.
   b. body.
   c. mind and body.

2. The triathlon is a combination of _____ sports.
   a. two
   b. three
   c. eight

3. People need up to _____ months to train for a competition.
   a. 8
   b. 7
   c. 6

4. The first Ironman competition was held in Hawaii in
   a. 1970.
   b. 1978.
   c. 1982.

5. Julie Moss won the "Ironman" in
   a. 1982.
   b. 1983.
   c. 1985.

6. People can compete in a triathlon
   a. at a young age.
   b. at an old age.
   c. at any age.

B. Answer the following information questions. In the reading, underline the words that support your answer. Write the question number in the margin.

1. What does it take to compete in the triathlon?

2. Why did athletes introduce a three-sport race into their training?

3. How did the Ironman become famous?

4. How did Julie Moss finish her first competition?

5. What are two positive qualities of triathletes?

Check your answers. Take turns reading your answers with a partner. Refer to the reading in cases where you disagree.

NOTE TAKING

Find the information to complete this chart from the reading. Write the details in note form, as shown in the example (boldface) below.

Sport:	Swimming	Biking	Running
Distance:	**2.4 miles (3.84 km)**		
Training:			
Cost:			expensive

Work with a partner to compare your information. Write two questions about the information. For example, you could ask, "Which sport covers the longest distance?"

1. _____

2. _____

After Reading

APPLYING THE INFORMATION: PROBLEM SOLVING

Use the information from the reading and your own experience to complete this activity. Read the following stories and decide whom to pick for a triathlon team. Put the candidates in order from best (1) to last (3). Be sure to have the reasons for your choice.

A. Jed Allen is fifty years old. He is a single father with two teenage children. He likes to swim with his son and to bicycle with his daughter. He trains with them 3 days a week. When he was a university student, he won medals in marathon running. He is the president of a large clothing company. He would like to join the team. He thinks that his children would enjoy training with him as he prepares.

B. Jerry Fox is twenty years old. He is a medical student and wins honors in his university program. Jerry loves swimming and biking. He gets up at 6:00 every day and works out in the gym for 2 hours before school. Jerry's girlfriend is a triathlete. He wants to join the team so that they can train together.

C. Marian Lowe is 40 years old. She is a mother and wife. She and her husband have a successful computer business. Marian is a champion swimmer and was a member of a national swim team. She likes a challenge and spends her weekends bicycling with her family. She runs with a group of friends. They started to do triathlete training two years ago. She is the best in her club.

_____

Work with a partner or in a small group and discuss your choices. Decide whom you will choose to join the team. Complete the following chart. Be prepared to explain the reasons for your choices.

	Choice	*Pros (Reasons good on the team)*	*Cons (Reasons against)*
1.	_____	_____	_____
2.	_____	_____	_____
3.	_____	_____	_____

Vocabulary Building

ANTONYMS

Antonyms are two words that have opposite meanings, such as *good* and *bad*. **Match each word in Column A with its antonym in Column B.**

Column A

_____ 1. finish

_____ 2. expensive

_____ 3. run

_____ 4. get up

_____ 5. lose

_____ 6. married

_____ 7. positive

Column B

a. single

b. cheap

c. crawl

d. negative

e. win

f. fall down

g. start

Use three of those pairs of words (the word and its opposite) in sentences of your own.

1. _____

2. _____

3. _____

WORD FORM

In English, some nouns have an *-ing* ending. You will find examples of some of these kinds of nouns in the reading. Complete each of the following statements with the correct form of the word.

1. bicycle / bicycling

   I like _____ because it is such great exercise.

2. train / training

   You have to do a lot of _____ if you want to finish the race.

3. race / racing

In her training, she would _____ for 10 km each day.

4. swim / swimming

For me, _____ is the hardest part of the event.

5. run / running

He was so tired that he didn't think he would be able to

_____ up the last hill.

Check your answers. Take turns reading your sentences with a partner.

VOCABULARY IN CONTEXT

Complete each sentence with one of the words from the list. Underline the part of the sentence that helped you to choose your answer.

a. after   b. before   c. brought   d. equipment

e. finish   f. salary   g. test   h. tried

1. Top-quality _____, such as shoes and bicycles, is expensive.

2. The triathlon is a _____ that measures both the body and the mind.

3. She lost the race, but she _____ again and won.

4. She tried to _____ the race, but she fell down before the end.

5. He _____ this sport to people in his new home.

6. She earned a good _____ in her new job.

7. She felt nervous _____ the race started but very good

_____ it was over.

Check your answers. Work with a partner and take turns reading the completed sentences.

Expanding Your Language

SPEAKING

Oral Presentation: Choose a sport that is interesting or new or an athlete who is good at his or her sport. To prepare your presentation, follow these steps.

1. Decide who or what you will present (the subject of your presentation). Find out whether the topic is interesting to your audience. Try to choose an unusual or little-known subject.

2. Read about the subject. To find information, check in the library for access to an online encyclopedia or ask your teacher.

3. Take notes of the information you want to present. Make an outline of these facts, as in the following example:

Subject of Presentation: Jackrabbit Johanson

Who was he:	▪ Canadian cross-country skier born in Norway
What did he do:	▪ came to Quebec, Canada, in the 1950s ▪ lived with his family in a cabin north of Montreal ▪ lived in the woods; no electricity or running water ▪ made the first country-country ski trail ▪ brought first group of skiers to the area
What did he accomplish:	▪ made more than 100 km of trails for people to ski on ▪ made the sport popular in Canada ▪ taught many young people how to cross-country ski ▪ improved the practice of the sport ▪ led an annual 100 km race ▪ lived until 111 years old
Why I chose this topic:	▪ lived an unusual life; close to nature ▪ developed a sport that many people enjoy today ▪ lived a long, purposeful life

4. Practice your presentation. Write four questions for people to answer after your presentation.

CHAPTER 11

Looking for Excitement

Chapter Openers

DISCUSSION QUESTIONS: THRILLING SPORTS

Think about these questions. Discuss your ideas with a partner or with a small group.

1. What sports are popular to practice outdoors in the winter?

2. What sports are popular to practice in the city?

3. What are the differences between indoor and outdoor sports? Which do you prefer? Give reasons for your choice.

4. Why do you think that such sports as snowboarding or rock climbing are becoming more popular?

PAIRED READINGS

Choose one of the readings about two popular sports in North America today. Work with a partner who is reading the same story. Read and find out about the sport and whom it attracts.

■ ■
_____

Reading 1: In the Winter: The Thrill of Snowboarding

PREDICTING: GETTING INFORMATION FROM ILLUSTRATIONS

Work with a partner and compare the similarities and differences between these two pictures.

1. What are people doing?

2. How are people dressed?

3. Which sport would you prefer? Explain your reasons.

UNDERSTANDING THE MAIN IDEAS

Read all of the paragraphs that follow. Write the letter of the paragraph that best fits each of these main ideas.

1. _____ On the ski slopes, people have different reactions to snowboarders.

2. _____ Skiers are learning about how to use snowboards on the mountains.

3. _____ Snowboarding is now becoming a very popular sport in North America for young and old.

UNDERSTANDING DETAILS

Answer the questions after each paragraph. In the story, underline the facts that support your answer. Write the question number in the margin of the reading.

A New Sport Catches On

A. In the winter, skiing is traditionally a popular sport for people of all ages who like to be outdoors. People take their ski equipment and head for the mountains. But these days, skiers are not the only people on the hills. Snowboarders are joining the skiers for some winter thrills. Snowboarding is fun and exciting. It is like surfing on the snow. Snowboards are wide, like surfboards, and there are places on the boards to strap them to your feet. You stand on the board and ride the snow like the surfers who ride the ocean waves. Snowboarders move back and forth in wide curves. Snowboarders like to jump and turn as they speed down the mountains.

_____

1. Where do skiers and snowboarders go in the winter?

_____

_____

2. Why do people like snowboarding?

   _____

   _____

3. What do snowboards look like?

   _____

   _____

4. How do people ride a snowboard?

   _____

   _____

5. What do people like to do on snowboards?

   _____

   _____

B.   The first people to try snowboarding were young people in their teens
     and twenties. They liked the new sport because it was fast and chal-
     lenging. They could do special tricks on the board, such as turning over
     or jumping over bumps in the snow. These young snowboarders wore
     special clothes and used a special vocabulary to talk about their moves.
     For example, they called themselves "shredders" because they would
     shred, or tear up, the snow as they moved. When snowboarding first
     started, skiers did not like the young "shredders." The skiers didn't like
     the snowboarders' fast and unusual movements. Sometimes, snow-
     boarders damaged the ski paths and made it dangerous for the skiers
     coming down the mountain. Skiers didn't understand the language and
     the attitude of snowboarders. Some ski resorts banned snowboarders
     and didn't allow them on the hills, because of the skiers' complaints.

_____

1. Who were the first people to try snowboarding?

   _____

   _____

2. Why did they like snowboarding?

   _____

   _____

3. What did snowboarders wear, and how did they talk?

   _____

   _____

4. How did skiers feel about snowboarders, and why did they feel
    this way?

   _____

   _____

5. What did ski resorts do, and why did they do this?

   _____

   _____

C.   But today, things are different. Snowboarding is becoming more and more popular. Some people think that in the next 5 years, 50 percent of the people who visit ski resorts will be snowboarders. Now snowboarders can compete internationally because it has become an Olympic sport. And it's no longer a sport that's just for the young. Now when you visit the ski slopes, you'll see people of all ages who are learning to snowboard. For example, there are lessons for mothers and businesspeople. The average age for people who are learning is forty, and the number of people trying the sport is up 200 percent. Now ski resorts welcome snowboarders to share the hills with skiers.

_____

1. What do people think will happen in the next 5 years?

    _____

    _____

2. Where can snowboarders compete?

    _____

    _____

3. Who can learn to snowboard?

    _____

    _____

4. What is the average age for people who learn snowboarding?

    _____

    _____

5. a. How do ski resorts now feel about snowboarders?

    _____

    _____

   b. What is the reason that ski resorts welcome snowboarders?

    _____

    _____

Work with a partner. Take turns reading the questions and answers to each other. Refer to the reading if your answers are different.

RECAPPING THE STORY

Note Taking: Listing the Facts

In note form, list the facts of the information from each of the paragraphs. To make your notes, reread the information, and underline the key words in the story.

Example: In the <u>winter, skiing</u> is traditionally a <u>popular sport</u> <u>for people of all ages</u> who like to be <u>outdoors</u>. People take their <u>ski equipment</u> and head for the <u>mountains</u>. But these days, skiers are not the only people on the hills. <u>Snowboarders</u> are <u>joining</u> the <u>skiers</u> for some winter thrills. <u>Snowboarding</u> is <u>fun</u> and <u>exciting</u>. It is like <u>surfing on the snow</u>.

Use the key words you underlined to make an outline, a plan that shows the order of the information, of the facts, as in the following example:

Notes: Paragraph A
    1. skiing
        popular sport for people of all ages
        outdoors, winter
    2. snowboarding
        fun and exciting
        surfing on the snow

Work with a partner who read the same information. Take turns explaining the information in your outline for each of the paragraphs. Use your notes to help you remember the facts, but do not read your outline. Tell your partner as much as you can remember. Ask for help if you forget or give incorrect information. Ask your partner to retell the information.

REACTING TO THE STORY

Discuss these questions with your partner.

1. Would you ever try snowboarding? Why or why not?

2. What kind of people do you think should or shouldn't try snowboarding?

3. Do you think that snowboarding will continue to be popular?

4. Is snowboarding dangerous? What safety rules should resorts make for the people who come to ski or snowboard?

Reading 2:
In the City: Climbing the Wall

PREDICTING: GETTING INFORMATION FROM ILLUSTRATIONS

Work with a partner and compare the similarities and differences between these two pictures. Together, answer these questions:

1. What are these people doing?

2. Where are they?

3. What equipment are they using?

4. How do they feel as they are climbing?

5. How do they feel when they finish?

6. Why do you think people like this sport? Would you like it?

7. Would you like indoor or outdoor climbing?

UNDERSTANDING THE MAIN IDEAS

Read all of the paragraphs. Write the letter of the paragraph that best fits each of these main ideas.

1. _____ There are many reasons why climbing is good for you.

2. _____ Climbing the wall is not a very difficult sport if you have the right equipment and attitude.

3. _____ More people are finding out that they can learn to climb in the city.

UNDERSTANDING DETAILS

Answer the questions after each paragraph. In the story, underline the facts that support your answer. Write the question number in the margin of the reading.

Overcoming Fear

A. Rock climbing is a popular sport. Many Americans are putting on climbing boots and other climbing equipment to walk up the side of a mountain. How did this sport become so popular? Where do people learn the skill of climbing? Many people learn outdoors in parks or other places. But if you think that you have to go to the mountains to learn how to climb, you're wrong. Many Americans are learning to climb in city gyms. Here, people are learning on special climbing walls. The climbing wall goes straight up and has small holding places for hands and feet.

1. What do you need to wear to go climbing?

   _____

   _____

2. Where do many people go to learn the skill of climbing?

   a. outdoors _____

   b. indoors _____

3. What do climbing walls look like?

   _____

   _____

B.   How do people climb the wall? To climb, you need special shoes and a harness around your chest to hold you. There are ropes to attach to your harness. The ropes hold you in place so that you don't fall. A beginner's wall is usually about 15 feet high, and you climb straight up. There are small pieces of metal that stick out for you to stand on and hold on to. Sometimes it's easy to see the next piece of metal. Sometimes, it's not. The most difficult part is to control your fear. Fear of falling is a normal human reaction, so it's difficult not to feel fear. But when you move away from the wall, the harness and the ropes hold you, and you begin to feel safe. You move slowly until you reach the top. At the top, the teacher slowly releases the rope, and then you slide back to the floor. Your arms and legs feel tired, but you feel great. Learning to climb is not very difficult.

1. What equipment do you need to climb?

_____

_____

2. What are the ropes for?

_____

_____

3. Where do you put your hands and feet on the wall?

_____

_____

4. What is the most difficult part and why?

_____

_____

5. What happens when you move away from the wall?

_____

_____

6. What happens at the end, and how do you feel?

_____

_____

C.   Climbing attracts people because it is good exercise. You don't have to be a superathlete to climb the wall. It's good exercise for almost anyone. You use your whole body, especially your arms and legs. This sport gives your body a complete workout. When you climb, you strengthen your mind as well as your body. This is a sport for people who like a challenge.

_____

1. Why do people like to climb?

_____

_____

2. What kind of people can be good climbers?

_____

_____

3. What parts of the body do you use in climbing?

_____

_____

4. Why is this sport good for you?

_____

_____

Work with a partner. Take turns reading the questions and answers. Refer to the information in the reading if you have different answers.

RECAPPING THE STORY

Note Taking: Listing the Facts

In note form, list the facts of the information from each of the paragraphs. To make your notes, reread the information, and underline the key words from the information.

Example: <u>Rock climbing</u> is a <u>popular</u> sport. Many Americans are putting on <u>climbing boots</u> and other climbing <u>equipment</u> to <u>walk up</u> the <u>side of a mountain</u>. <u>How</u> did this sport become so popular? <u>Where do people learn</u> the skill of climbing? Many people learn <u>outdoors in parks or other places</u>.

From the words you underlined, make an outline, a plan that shows the order of the information, of the facts, as in the following example:

Notes: Paragraph A
     1. Rock climbing
        popular
        climbing boots and equipment
        walk up ... side of a mountain
     2. How ... become popular
     3. Where do people learn
        outdoors in parks or other places

Work with a partner who read the same information. Take turns explaining the information in your outline for each of the paragraphs. Use your notes to help you remember the facts, but do not read your outline. Tell your partner as much as you can remember. Ask for help if you forget or give incorrect information. Ask your partner to retell the information.

REACTING TO THE STORY

Discuss these questions with your partner.

1. Would you try indoor or outdoor climbing? Why or why not?

2. What kind of people do you think should or shouldn't try climbing?

3. What do you think is easy or difficult about climbing? Why is this sport popular?

4. Do you agree with people who think that climbing is dangerous? Why or why not?

After Reading

COMPARING THE INFORMATION

Work with a partner who read a different story. Together, ask each other questions, and use your notes to complete the chart.

Questions	Snowboarding	Climbing
1. What do you have to do to learn this sport?		
2. What kind of equipment do you need to have?		
3. What kind of people can learn this sport?		
4. Where and when can you practice this sport?		
5. Is this an Olympic sport?		
6. What is the challenge of this sport?		
7. Why is this sport popular?		

From the information in the chart, circle the things that are similar about these two sports. Prepare to explain this information to the class.

ROLE PLAY

Think of a new sport, such as beach volleyball or wind surfing, that you think is fun to do. Give four or five reasons you think a person should try this new sport. Explain the sport—how you play, what the rules are, where you play, what equipment you need, and so on—and write your short list of reasons.

For example: It's easy to learn this sport. It's a really fun sport if you like a challenge. It's not expensive to play. You can meet new people.

Work with a partner and take turns convincing each other to try this new sport. Ask questions about the sport to find out as many details as possible.

Vocabulary Building

VOCABULARY IN CONTEXT

A. Complete each statement with one of the adjectives from the readings. In the sentence, underline the words that helped you to make your choice. Circle the word you chose.

1. She was moving at such speed down the mountain with

   _____ and unusual movements.

2. The _____ part of this sport is learning to control the fear.

3. People learn to climb on _____ _____ walls.

4. The _____ age for people who try this sport is rising.

5. Skiing is a very _____ sport for people who like to be outdoors in the winter.

6. This sport gives your body a _____ workout.

7. Snowboards are _____ like surfboards.

B. Jigsaw Sentences: *When* is a word that introduces a condition or a time period in which an action takes place. *When* can begin a sentence, or it can be within a sentence. Use your understanding of the ideas to complete these sentences.

Match the beginning of each sentence in Column A with the ending that fits it best in Column B.

Column A	Column B
_____ 1. When you move away from the wall,	a. skiers didn't like the young "shredders."
_____ 2. When you climb,	b. you'll see that people of all ages are learning to snowboard.
_____ 3. When you visit the ski slopes,	c. you strengthen your mind as well as your body.
_____ 4. When snowboarding first started,	d. the harness and the ropes hold you, and you begin to feel safe.

Check your answers. Work with a partner. Take turns reading your answers.

Expanding Your Language

SPEAKING

A. Preparing a Questionnaire: Find out what the most popular indoor and outdoor sports are among the students in your class. Choose one of the topics to answer. Answer the questions yourself. Then interview two other people and write notes of their answers.

Questions	You	Student A	Student B
Indoor sports			
1. What sport do you practice?			
2. Where do you go?			
3. How often?			
4. What equipment do you need?			
5. What training do you need?			
6. How expensive is this sport?			
7. How challenging is it?			

Questions	You	Student A	Student B
Outdoor sports			
1. What sport do you practice?			
2. Where do you go?			
3. How often?			
4. What equipment do you need?			
5. What training do you need?			
6. How expensive is this sport?			
7. How challenging is it?			

Form a group and compare your information. Make a report of your group's answers to present to the whole class.

B. Two-Minute Taped Talk: Record a 2-minute audiotape about one of the sports you learned about in this chapter. To make your tape, follow the steps on page 60.

CHAPTER 12

Training for the Olympics Today: What Does It Take?

Chapter Openers

GETTING INFORMATION FROM A CHART

A. Use the information from the chart to answer the following questions about the Olympics then and now.

Year:	*1896*	*1996*
Number of athletes:	300	10,000
Number of countries:	15	190
Events:	43	271
Sports:	9	29
Who is allowed to compete:	Only amateurs	Amateurs and professionals
International press coverage:	Very little	On live television around the world
Training times:	A few months; part time	All year; full time

1. Compare the number of athletes at the Olympic Games in the past and in recent years.

2. How many more countries now come to the modern Olympics?

3. What kinds of athletes were allowed in the Games in 1896, and how is that different today?

4. What kind of press coverage do Olympic athletes get today, and how is that different from the past?

B. Discuss your answers with a partner. Then share your ideas about the following questions.

1. Why do athletes go to the Olympics?

2. How much time and money does an athlete have to spend to get to the Olympics?

3. In comparison with athletes in the past, what do today's athletes know about
   a. how much time to train?
   b. what kind of food to eat?
   c. what kind of equipment to use?
   d. how to prepare themselves mentally?

Understanding and Exploring Reading

PREDICTING

Read the following statements. Write *P* for statements you think are about athletes of the past and *T* for statements about today's athletes. Write *B* if you think that the statement is true for both.

_____ 1. Athletes train part time for the Olympics.

_____ 2. Sports psychologists help athletes improve through mental training.

_____ 3. Athletes train without special equipment or coaches.

_____ 4. Athletes train for a long time.

_____ 5. Athletes show determination and self-sacrifice.

_____ 6. Athletes know the science of how the body produces energy.

_____ 7. Athletes use video cameras to study their performance.

_____ 8. Athletes can improve their performances in small amounts over time.

_____ 9. Athletes represent their countries at the games.

Compare your answers with a partner. Try to agree on the same answer. Check your answers after you finish the reading. Make any changes necessary.

▪▪ *Reaching for Olympic Gold: Past and Present* ▪▪

A. In the past, people who participated in the Olympics worked on their training part time. Many athletes trained at a university. They practiced their sport while they were studying. Some trained on their own, without special coaches or equipment. They spent only a few months of daily training before the Games. For the athletes who competed in past Olympics, training was an individual responsibility. Like the athletes of today, to reach the top of any sport, athletes needed determination and self-sacrifice. It takes physical and mental training. The goals and aspirations of today's athletes are no different from those of the past. But today, training for the Olympics is a full-time job. Training today is different from the way it was in the past.

B. Today's athletes have much more knowledge about how their bodies perform than the athletes of the past did. Science can now show us how our bodies produce energy. But the amount of energy depends on how long a person trains. Today's athletes have to train for a long time to improve. Coaches can help athletes make important training decisions. Athletes need to follow a schedule and to keep working continuously at improving. They have to get the right amount of sleep and to eat the right food. Sometimes, they have to get up early in the morning and train for hours before going to school or work. Coaches use video cameras and computers to record an athlete's movements. With their coaches, athletes analyze and study how to move their bodies so that they will improve their performance. The improvement they make is small. But at the Olympics, small improvements can make a big difference. A few seconds is all that separates getting a medal and not getting a medal.

C. Today, athletes are learning how to use their minds as well as their bodies. Sports psychologists help athletes improve their performances through mental training by teaching them how to concentrate. They show athletes how to raise their self-esteem and their motivation. They can teach them how to visualize, or "see," themselves winning. Athletes can learn these skills and improve their performances. Elizabeth Manley is a good example of an athlete who improved with the help of psychological training. Elizabeth was a talented figure skater. She skated well at practice. She could do difficult jumps. But she didn't do her best at competitions. It was very frustrating. She lost her confidence. Then she decided to use a sports psychologist. The psychologist helped her to imagine herself giving a perfect performance. She trained with the psychologist for a year before the 1988 Winter Olympics competition. Before she went on the ice at the Olympics, she practiced her routine in her mind. The mental work paid off. She had a silver medal at the end of the competition. Today, many athletes use psychological training to get the competitive edge they need to win.

UNDERSTANDING THE MAIN IDEA

Write the letter of the paragraph that best fits each of these main ideas.

_____ 1. Sports psychologists can help athletes to do their best.

_____ 2. Olympic training today is very different from the way it was in the past.

_____ 3. Athletes today need to know a lot about how to train for their sport.

IDENTIFYING SUPPORTING POINTS AND DETAILS

Read each statement and decide whether it is a supporting (sub) point or a detail. Refer to the reading to help you decide. Write S for supporting points and *D* for details.

■ *READING TIP: Some information, such as sub, or supporting, points of a main idea, is more general than other information, such as dates, numbers, or other details. Noticing this type of difference will help you to relate ideas to one another as you read.*

———— 1. Today's athletes have to train for a long time to improve.

———— 2. Sometimes, they have to get up early in the morning and train for hours before going to school or work.

———— 3. A few seconds are all that separate getting a medal or not getting a medal.

———— 4. At the Olympics, small improvements can make a big difference.

———— 5. Sports psychologists help athletes to improve their performances through mental training.

———— 6. They teach athletes how to concentrate.

Compare your answers with a partner.

USING INFORMATION TO COMPLETE A CHART

Find information in paragraphs A and B to complete this chart. Write the details in note form, as shown in the following example (*italics*).

Athletes in the Past	Athletes Today
Worked on their training part time	*Train for a long time to improve*
Trained at university	*Follow a schedule and keep training continuously*

Work with a partner. Check to make sure that your information is the same. Take turns telling about the training of athletes today and in the past.

After Reading

APPLYING THE INFORMATION: PROBLEM SOLVING

Read the following short interviews with young athletes and decide whether they should

1. get the help of a sports psychologist.

2. get the help of a training coach.

Give reasons based on the interview and information from the first reading.

INTERVIEW A

Interviewer: How long have you been training?
    Athlete: Twelve years. I started when I was five years old.
Interviewer: Will you compete in the next Olympics?
    Athlete: Yes, I am on the team. We're training now.
Interviewer: I watched your training session. It was wonderful; you did everything perfectly.
    Athlete: Thanks. But I still have to work hard.
Interviewer: What is your goal; what is the most difficult part for you?
    Athlete: The most difficult part isn't the training. It's the competition.
Interviewer: What happens in the competitions?
    Athlete: I'm not sure. Sometimes, I freeze and my performance isn't good enough. I do better in training.
Interviewer: Do you need to spend more time training?
    Athlete: I'm not sure. I spend 4 hours a day now. Maybe I need something else.

Your suggestion: _____

Reasons why: _____

INTERVIEW B

Interviewer: How long have you been training?
   Athlete: Twelve years. I started when I was five years old.
Interviewer: Will you compete in the next Olympics?
   Athlete: Yes, I am on the team. We're training now.
Interviewer: I watched your training session. It was wonderful; you did everything perfectly.
   Athlete: Thanks. But I still have to work hard.
Interviewer: What is your goal; what is the most difficult part for you?
   Athlete: The most difficult part is making improvement in my time. I want to finish at least 30 seconds faster.
Interviewer: What happens in the competitions?
   Athlete: I need to have more energy at the end. It's the last minute or so that is difficult for me.
Interviewer: Do you need to spend more time training?
   Athlete: I'm not sure. I spend 4 hours a day now. Maybe I'm doing something wrong.

Your suggestion: _____

Reasons why: _____

Compare your suggestions with others. Be prepared to give the reasons for your suggestions.

DISCUSSION QUESTIONS: THE OLYMPIC EXPERIENCE

Think about these questions. Discuss your ideas with a partner or with a small group.

1. What are three important reasons that people become Olympic athletes?

2. What rewards do Olympic athletes enjoy?

3. What difficulties do Olympic athletes experience?

4. What problems have the Olympics had? What are the reasons for these problems?

5. What do you think will be the future of the Olympics?

Vocabulary Building

VOCABULARY IN CONTEXT

A. Past and Present: Decide whether the sentence needs a verb in the present or in the past or both. Write the correct form of the verb on the line provided. In the sentence, circle the words that helped you make your decision.

1. train

   Today, people _____ very differently from the way

   they _____ at the beginning of the century.

2. produce

   Unlike in the past, we now know a lot about how the body

   _____ energy.

3. go

   Before she _____ on the ice, she asked her coach to
   help her to concentrate.

4. take

   As in the past, it _____ years of hard work to reach
   the top of any sport.

5. teach

   Now they _____ athletes by using computers and
   video equipment. It's very different from the way that they

   _____ before.

Check your answers. Take turns reading your sentences.

B. Complete each sentence with one of the words from the following list. In the reading, underline the words that helped you to choose your answer.

a. competition   b. confidence   c. difference

d. improvement   e. knowledge   f. motivation

g. performance   h. self-esteem

1. The coach taught me not to think about the crowds of people watching but to concentrate on giving the best _____ I could.

2. I did very well at practice, but now I needed to do well at the _____.

3. He didn't do as well as he could have, because he lost _____ in himself.

4. I had the _____ to do well, but I worried that I hadn't spent enough time training.

5. The coach told her that she could make a small _____ in her game.

6. The _____ between his ability before he trained and after was amazing.

7. Today, we have much more _____ about what is going on in the body than we did before.

8. I needed to think well of myself and to raise my own _____.

Check your answers. Take turns reading your sentences.

Expanding Your Language

SPEAKING

Role Play: Work with a partner. Choose the role of an athlete and a sports psychologist or a training coach. Together, write out the conversation between these two people, based on the chapter readings and information of your own.

For example, the athlete could be looking for someone to help increase self-esteem and improve performance at competitions. Or an athlete could be looking for someone to help have a better result in training. Here is one example of how to start the conversation:

Athlete: I need help to do better when I have to compete. Can you help me?
Coach: I think I can help. I'm a sports psychologist.
Athlete: How can you help me?

1. **Together, practice your role plays with your partner. Prepare to present one of them to others in a small group.**

2. **Find another partner and take roles in each other's scenario.**

WRITING

Topic Writing: From the information in this chapter or based on your own interests, write about a topic of your choice or one of the following topics:

How Athletes of Today Train for their Sport
The Olympics in the Past

To write about your topic, follow these steps:

1. Decide on the topic of your writing. Make notes of the information you want to include in your writing. Make an outline using these facts. An outline showing the supporting points is shown in the following example.

   ■ Topic A. Olympic Training Today

        1. How many athletes and sports
        2. Training:
          a. Types
          b. Where
          c. How long
          d. Expense
        3. Problems

   ■ Topic B: Olympic Training in the Past

        1. How many athletes and sports
        2. Training:
          a. Where
          b. How long
          c. Expense
        3. Problems

2. Work with a partner. Use your outline to tell your partner what you plan to write about. Ask your partner whether the information is clear or whether you should add any ideas to make the information more complete.

3. Use your notes to help you organize your writing. Write as much as you can. Write in complete sentences. Refer to the exercise in Chapter 3, pages 34 and 35, to help write your sentences.

▮ Read On: Taking It Further

READING CLOZE

Use words from the unit as listed here to fill in the blanks in this paragraph.

a. best   b. better   c. earlier (2×)   d. free   e. hard

f. long   g. longer   h. many (2×)   i. older   j. young

What makes an athlete great? According to many coaches, athletes have to work (1) _____ and work (2) _____ hours to reach their goals. The (3) _____ an athlete works at training, the (4) _____ that athlete will be. Most athletes have to face (5) _____ demands. They often get up (6) _____ than most people. They also go to bed (7) _____ and do not go for a night out with friends very often. Many of the (8) _____ athletes start training when they are still young. These (9) _____ athletes can have (10) _____ problems as they get (11) _____. They haven't had enough time to learn how to manage their (12) _____ time or to develop other interests in their life.

Check your answers.

READING JOURNAL

Some very interesting stories have been written about famous athletes of the past, such as Muhammed Ali or Wayne Gretsky. You can find these and other stories in easy-reader texts that your teacher can suggest.

Choose a story about an athlete or a sport that you are interested in. Read the story and then use your reading journal to write some information about what you read. Prepare to tell a partner about the important facts of the story. Show your journal entries to your teacher.

WORD PLAY

Choose five to seven new words that you would like to learn from the readings in the unit. Try to choose words that are important, such as the nouns, verbs, and adjectives in a sentence. Make a list of these new words. Write a sentence using each of the words from your list. Underline the new word you used. Write the meaning of the word: a definition. Check the work with your teacher.

Work with a partner. Tell your partner the definition of the word, the first letter of its spelling, and the number of letters in the word. Ask your partner to guess the word and to give the correct spelling. Continue to give the letters of the word until your partner makes a correct guess.

Technology for Today's World

Nothing is impossible
— Lewis Mumford

Introducing *the* Topics

Much of what we use every day was invented in the last 20 to 30 years. It doesn't take long for us to become familiar with new technology. Then it doesn't take long for us to need it in our lives. Chapter 13 introduces a new way to grow food. Chapter 14 compares the pros and cons of the role of cell phones and e-mail in our daily lives. Chapter 15 shows one way that the Internet is bringing families closer.

Points of Interest

What kinds of technology do you think have greatly changed our world? Give as many ideas as you can.

CHAPTER 13

Food for the Twenty-First Century

Chapter Openers

QUESTIONNAIRE

Answer these questions for yourself. Ask two classmates these same questions.

Questions	You	Student A	Student B
1. What are your favorite foods?			
2. What are the various ways we process food to keep it fresh?			
3. What food can we grow today without soil and water (hydroponically)?			
4. What would you eat if you lived in a space colony?			
5. Where would your food come from?			
6. In the future, why will it be important to find new ways to grow and process food?			

Work with a partner. Take turns telling each other about the information you learned from your questionnaire.

Exploring and Understanding Reading

PREDICTING: AGREE/DISAGREE

Write *A* if you agree or *D* if you don't agree with the statements. Give the reasons for your answers.

_____ 1. We can grow food in space colonies.

_____ 2. We can grow lettuce and tomatoes in cold weather.

_____ 3. We need sunlight to grow food.

_____ 4. We can grow food by using chemicals.

_____ 5. We can make delicious meals without using meat.

PREVIEWING

Read the title and the first and last sentences of each paragraph in the reading. From the following list, check (✔) the ideas you expect to find out about in this reading.

I expect to find out about

_____ 1. growing food on the earth.

_____ 2. growing food in space colonies.

_____ 3. growing hydroponic vegetables.

_____ 4. making recipes with hydroponic foods.

_____ 5. making meals for fancy restaurants.

_____ 6. experiments with recipes for space-age meals.

Compare your choices with a partner. Try to agree on your answers. Read the complete article. Return to the preview list and change or add to the ideas you checked.

■■
_____

What's for Dinner?

A. Do you want something different for dinner? Try some space food. Scientists are experimenting with ways to grow food in space. Scientists think that in 20 or 30 years, astronauts will be able to live in space colonies off the planet. It's too expensive to carry food to feed people living in space colonies. People in space colonies will need to grow food for themselves. But how can they grow food without soil and sunlight?

B. Today, we already have hydroponic (hī´drə-pŏn´ĭk) vegetables. These are vegetables you can grow without soil. The food can grow in an artificial environment. In addition to sunlight, hydroponic farms can use artificial lights. Instead of soil, hydroponic farms can use special material, such as charcoal and mixtures of chemicals, to feed the plants. And in addition to a natural climate, most hydroponic farms often use greenhouses. Farmers know how to grow a few kinds of hydroponic vegetables. In winter, when it is too cold to grow vegetables outdoors, hydroponic farmers can grow such vegetables as lettuce, tomatoes, and cucumbers and many different herbs and spices. These products are in many super-markets. But in space, people will need to eat more than salad and spices. So scientists are learning how to grow hydroponic rice, beans, potatoes, and wheat. Scientists can even grow hydroponic melons and strawberries.

C.   Nutrition scientists at Cornell University in New York State are experi-menting with recipes that use these hydroponic vegetables. The National Aeronautics and Space Agency (NASA) is paying for this nutrition research. Some of the Cornell experiments are unusual. They make imi-tation meat dishes, such as carrot drumsticks, made from carrots, pep-pers, onions, garlic, herbs, and breadcrumbs, instead of chicken. They make dishes made from tofu and seitan (a wheat protein) instead of meat. How do these unusual foods taste? The scientists invite a group of taste testers into their laboratories. Every week, twenty-five people come to taste five different dishes. So far, they have tested 200 different recipes. The carrot drumstick dish was a hit. It rated an 8 out of 9. Perhaps soon, people will eat meals made from hydroponic vegetables that are truly out of this world.

UNDERSTANDING DETAILS

A. Circle the letter of the correct answer. In the reading, under-line the words that support your answer.

1. Scientists are experimenting with
   a. ways to grow food in space colonies.
   b. ways to grow food in the cold weather.
   c. ways to grow food in expensive restaurants.

2. It takes too much _____ to bring food to space colonies.
   a. time
   b. money
   c. work

3. To grow hydroponic vegetables, you need
   a. chemicals to feed the plants.
   b. sunlight and warm weather.
   c. soil to grow the plants in.

4. You can find hydroponic vegetables in
   a. space laboratories.
   b. outdoor gardens.
   c. many supermarkets.

5. Scientists are experimenting with recipes that use
   a. vegetables instead of meat.
   b. chicken instead of tofu.
   c. chicken drumsticks.

6. Scientists invite _____ to try out their unusual recipes.
   a. taste testers
   b. NASA
   c. farmers

B. Answer the following questions. Write the question number in the margin where you found the information for your answer.

1. Why do scientists want to grow food in space?

   _____

   _____

2. To grow hydroponic vegetables, what do people use instead of soil, sunlight, and a natural climate?

   a. _____

   b. _____

   c. _____

3. What do hydroponic farmers grow when it is cold outside?

   _____

   _____

4. What kinds of hydroponic vegetables are produced now? What will people need in space?

	Hydroponic Vegetables Now	*Hydroponic Vegetables for Space Colonies*
a.	_____	_____
b.	_____	_____
c.	_____	_____
d.	_____	_____

5. What are scientists at Cornell University doing? Explain and give some examples.

_____

_____

6. a. Who comes to the laboratory every week?

_____

   b. What do they do?

_____

   c. What did they decide?

_____

Work with a partner. Take turns reading the questions and answers. Refer to the reading if you have different answers.

After Reading

APPLYING THE INFORMATION: MAKING AN ARGUMENT

Apply the information from the reading and from your own experience to give your opinion about the topic of this conversation.

Art: I tasted the most delicious food at Cornell today.

Judy: What was it?

Art: Carrot drumsticks.

Judy: Sounds strange. What's that?

Art: It's a vegetarian dish made from carrots, peppers, onions, garlic, herbs, and breadcrumbs, instead of chicken.

Judy: Why are they making this food?

Art: To try out recipes that people cook from food that they can grow out in space.

Judy: Is that very practical? Are you planning to join a space colony?

Art: You never know.

Judy: It sounds like a waste of money.

Art: I don't agree. Just 50 years, ago no one would have imagined all of the things we can do today. And some of the food we use every day, such as freeze-dried drinks, were developed as part of the space program.

Judy: But there are so many important things that we need to do here on Earth.

Art: Sure, but hydroponic food is good for us to grow on Earth, too. I think that the technology that comes from the space program benefits our daily life. Don't you?

1. What are Art and Judy arguing about?

   _____

2. What arguments can you think of *in favor* of the technological developments, such as hydroponic food, for the space program?

   _____

3. What arguments can you think of *against* these space research programs?

   _____

Share your ideas with a partner or with others in a small group. Be prepared to present your ideas to the class.

Vocabulary Building

VOCABULARY IN CONTEXT

A. Complete each sentence with one of the words from the following list. In the sentence, underline the words that helped you make your choice.

a. artificial   b. hydroponic   c. imitation   d. nutritional

e. unusual

1. You can find fresh _____ vegetables in the supermarket even in the winter.

2. She offered me some new and _____ dish that I had never tasted before.

3. The _____ meat tasted so real that I couldn't believe it was actually tofu.

4. NASA is paying for the _____ research that is developing food for people living in space colonies.

5. They used chemicals and created an _____ environment to grow the food they needed for the winter.

You can find the words *instead of* used in this reading to show that one thing can replace something else.

B. Complete the following sentences, using words from the reading. Use the meaning of the other words in the sentence to help you make a good guess.

1. Hydroponic farms use _____ instead of sunlight.

2. Instead of _____, hydroponic farms use special mixtures of chemicals.

3. Hydroponic farms can use greenhouses instead of a

   _____.

4. They can use _____ and _____ instead of meat.

In English, *but* links ideas that are different within the same sentence. An example of this is, "I don't have any meat, but I do have fish for supper."

C. Complete two of the sentences from the preceding list, using *but* to express the contrast.

1. Hydroponic farms don't use sunlight, but they use

   _____.

2. They don't use meat, but _____.

Check your answers. Take turns reading your answers.

Expanding Your Language

Choose story A, which follows, or story B, which is in the Exercise section of the book. Student A works with story A. Student B works with story B on page E-3. Complete the following steps.

1. Read the information questions about your story.
2. Read the story to find the main idea.
3. Underline the important facts that give the answers to the questions.
4. To compare the facts you underlined, work with a partner who read the same story.
5. Take turns asking and answering each other's questions.
6. Write your answers in note form.
7. Use your notes and take turns explaining as much of the story as you can.

Information Questions

1. Who developed this technology?

2. What is it used for?

3. How does it work?

4. What are the benefits?

5. Where is it used?

■ ■

Story A: Wheeling Water

South African architect Hans Hendrikse and his brother Piet, a civil engineer, have invented a new type of wheel. They made a round, thick drum with a hole in the middle. You can fill the drum with water, screw on the lid, and roll the drum along the ground. You can pull the drum with a rope that goes through the middle. With the drum, it is easier to carry water than by the old method of carrying it in buckets or in jars on backs. The brothers called their invention the Q-Drum. You can get the drum in 50- and 70-liter sizes. The invention is now used in Kenya, Ethiopia, Tanzania, Namibia, and South Africa.

RETELLING THE STORY

1. **Work with a partner who read a different story. Explain your story to each other. Use the illustrations to help you explain. Ask and answer each other's questions.**

2. **Together, make a list of the similarities and differences between your two stories.**

3. **Share your ideas with your classmates.**

4. **Use the questions and answers to help you write about each of the stories.**

CHAPTER 14

New Ways to Keep in Touch

Chapter Openers

DISCUSSION QUESTIONS: ADVANTAGES AND DISADVANTAGES

Think about these questions. Discuss your ideas with a partner or in a small group.

1. When do you talk on the phone? For what purposes?

2. Would you use a cell phone? Why or why not?

3. What are the advantages and disadvantages of cell phones?

4. When and how often do you send and receive mail?

5. Would you use the Internet to send or receive mail?

6. What are the advantages and disadvantages of e-mail?

PAIRED READINGS

"Keep in touch." Today, it's so easy to do. In fact, with the advances in today's communications systems, we can keep in touch almost all the time. These are readings about the newest means of communicating. Choose one of the readings and find out the advantages and disadvantages of cell phones or e-mail.

■■
_____

Reading 1: Cell Phones: The Pros and Cons

PREDICTING FROM GRAPHS

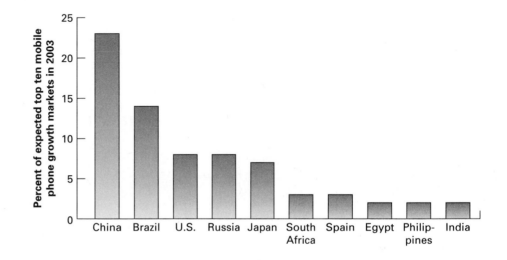

Look at the graph and answer these questions.

1. Where will cell phones be most popular in the year 2003?

_____

2. Do you think that cell phone use is increasing or decreasing? Explain the reasons for your answers.

_____

UNDERSTANDING THE MAIN IDEAS

Read both of the paragraphs. Then write a sentence that expresses the main idea of each paragraph.

A. _____

B. _____

UNDERSTANDING DETAILS

Answer the questions after each paragraph. In the story, underline the facts that support your answer. Write the question number in the margin.

Cell Phones: A Communications Revolution

A. Do you have to be at home to get a phone call? Not anymore. With a cell (short for cellular) phone, you can call people and receive calls anytime and anywhere. Cell phones use both radio waves and telephone lines.

You can get two kinds of phones: analog or digital. Some phones combine both types in one. With today's technology, you can have call waiting (to receive a call while you are already talking) and call display, which shows you, on your cell phone, the name of the caller. The cell phone can be your home office. You can send and receive faxes (short for facsimiles, such as documents and other printed material) and make notes to yourself on the phone. Cell phones are getting smaller and cheaper. People like the convenience of being able to call anytime from any location. You can use your cell phone to reach people anywhere in the world. Cell phones are also good in an emergency if you need to call for help.

_____

1. How easy is it to call people and receive calls with a cell phone?

   _____

   _____

2. What kinds of cell phones are there, and what do they use to work?

   _____

   _____

3. a. What is call waiting? _____

   b. What is call display? _____

4. What home office jobs can you do with a cell phone?

   a. _____

   b. _____

5. What are three ways that cell phones are beneficial?

   a. _____

   b. _____

   c. _____

B.   But is it all good news? Not always. Cell phones don't operate well when the battery is low. When a communications satellite failed in 1998, some users lost their phone service. Cell phones are dangerous to use when you drive. More and more car accidents happen while people are talking on their cell phones. Cell phone conversations are not private. People can listen in to other people's conversations when they are talking on cell phones. They do this by using a scanner that can pick up the same radio frequency used for the calls. People don't like to hear cell phones ringing when they are at the movies or in a class at school. And people don't like to have to listen to other people's private phone conversations while they are traveling on the bus or standing in line at the supermarket. Last, but not least, some cell phone companies charge quite a bit of money for using the service during certain times. Cell phones can be useful, but they can be expensive, and they can be annoying.

_____

1. When do cell phones not operate well?

    _____

    _____

2. What happened to some cell phone users in 1998?

    _____

    _____

3. Why are cell phones dangerous to use when you drive?

    _____

    _____

4. When do people not like to hear cell phones ringing?

    _____

    _____

5. When do people not want to listen to phones ringing or private phone conversations?

    _____

    _____

Work with a partner. Take turns reading the questions and answers to each other. Refer to the reading if your answers are different.

RECAPPING THE STORY: HIGHLIGHTING

Work with a partner who read the same information. Together, highlight the important facts in both paragraphs. Then use the information to complete this note-taking chart about cell phones.

> **■ READING TIP:**
> *Highlighting is a useful strategy for finding and remembering facts and important ideas you read. To highlight, use a colored highlighting pen to mark information. Be careful to mark only the information you want to tell your partner. Use the underlining you did to answer the questions to help you find the information to highlight.*

Questions	Facts
1. How do they work?	
2. Where can they work?	
3. What can you do with them?	
4. What are the advantages?	
5. What are the disadvantages?	

Practice telling the information to your partner. Try not to read the notes as you speak. Ask for help if you forget or give incorrect information. Ask your partner to retell the information.

REACTING TO THE STORY

A. Make a list of three or four advantages and disadvantages of cell phones. Use the information from the reading and some of your own ideas. Write your ideas in note form, as shown in the example (in italic).

Advantages	Disadvantages
1. *People can call anytime*	*Works only on batteries*
2.	
3.	
4.	

Work with a partner and share your ideas. Together, make a list of your best ideas to share with others.

B. Discuss these questions with others, and give the reasons for your answers.

1. Are there more advantages or disadvantages to using cell phones?

2. When would you use a cell phone? When wouldn't you use one?

3. How popular will cell phones become in the future?

Reading 2: E-Mail

GETTING INFORMATION FROM ILLUSTRATIONS

Look at the illustration and discuss these questions: When is e-mail useful? When is it annoying or not useful?

UNDERSTANDING THE MAIN IDEAS

Read both of the paragraphs. Write a sentence that expresses the main idea of each paragraph.

A. _____

B. _____

UNDERSTANDING DETAILS

Answer the questions after each paragraph. In the story, under-line the facts that support your answers. Write the question number in the margin of the reading.

Is E-Mail for Everyone?

A.   Do you want to send and receive e-mail (*e* for electronic)? It's easy to do. You can connect your computer and modem to a phone line. Then with a service provider, such as America Online, you can have an e-mail account and write, send, and receive messages. It's the most popular activity on the Internet. It is the most inexpensive way to communicate. You can send messages to people all over the world without paying for a long-distance call. With e-mail, you can send an instant message to anyone else who has an e-mail account—even the President of the United States. Many companies use e-mail for people in their offices or in other offices to communicate with one another. You can send the same message to fifty people or more. You can even work without having to go into the office; just dial up your office computer and transfer the files you need to your home computer. E-mail addresses are becoming as common as phone numbers. Many schools and universities give e-mail addresses to their students. You'll find lines to write your e-mail "address" on many official forms.

----

1. What can you do if you have an e-mail account?

   _____

   _____

2. Why is e-mail an inexpensive way to communicate to people in other cities, states, and countries?

   _____

   _____

3. Whom can you send e-mail to?

   _____

   _____

4. How many people can you send the same message to?

   _____

   _____

5. What are two ways that e-mail makes work easier?

   a. _____

   b. _____

6. How common are e-mail accounts becoming?

   _____

   _____

B.   But not everyone is happy about e-mail. Some e-mail is annoying junk mail. People don't want to read messages they aren't interested in. It can take time to check and clear your e-mail box. And in today's fast-paced world, we don't like to waste time. Sometimes, the lines are busy, and it's difficult to get a line and log on. Sometimes, the system crashes and can't be used. Some people feel that getting e-mail is not as satisfying as getting hand-written mail. These people like to receive handwritten letters and cards in the mail. There can be problems when people make the mistake of send-ing e-mail to the wrong person. In one case, an office worker complained about his boss in an e-mail to another employee. Then he pressed the wrong key to send it, and everyone in the office got the mail, including his boss. The office worker didn't lose his job, but it didn't help his problems at work. E-mail can be useful, but it can also make our lives more complicated.

1. What kind of e-mail messages do people not like to get?

   _____

   _____

2. How is e-mail wasteful of people's time?

   _____

   _____

3. Why do some people think that e-mail is not satisfying?

   _____

   _____

4. a. What kind of mistake can people make when they send e-mail?

   _____

   _____

   b. What is one example of this kind of mistake?

   _____

   _____

Work with a partner. Take turns reading the questions and answers. Refer to the reading if you have different answers.

RECAPPING THE STORY

■ *READING TIP: See page 169 for tips on highlighting.*

Work with a partner who read the same information. Together, highlight the important facts in both paragraphs. Then use the information to complete this note-taking chart on e-mail.

Questions	Facts
1. How does it work?	
2. Where can it be used?	
3. What can you do with it?	
4. What are the advantages?	
5. What are the disadvantages?	

Practice telling the information to your partner. Try not to read the notes as you speak. Ask for help if you forget or give incorrect information. Ask your partner to retell the information.

REACTING TO THE STORY

A. Make a list of three or four advantages and disadvantages of cell phones. Use the information from the reading and some of your own ideas. Write your ideas in note form, as shown in the example (in italic).

Advantages	Disadvantages
1. *People can send messages across long distances.*	*You might get junk mail.*
2.	
3.	
4.	

Work with a partner and share your ideas. Together, make a list of your best ideas to share with others.

B. Discuss these questions with others, and give the reasons for your answers.

1. Are there more advantages or disadvantages to using e-mail?

2. When would you want to use e-mail? When wouldn't you want to use it?

3. What do you think will be the future of e-mail?

After Reading

COMPARING THE INFORMATION

Work with a partner who read a different story. Use your notes and your charts to answer the following questions:

1. How does this communications technology work?

2. What are three advantages of this technology?

3. What are three disadvantages of this technology?

REACTING TO THE INFORMATION

Discuss the questions in the section "Reacting to the Story" for each reading. Explain whether, how, and when you would ever use these two communication tools.

Vocabulary Building

VOCABULARY IN CONTEXT

In English, technical terms are often explained by giving an explanation in words that follow. These explanations are set apart by special punctuation, such as commas (,) or parentheses ( ).

A. Look at the article, underline the technical words, and write the explanations for these terms:

1. e-mail _____

2. cell phones _____

3. faxes _____

4. call display _____

5. call waiting _____

Check your answers. Work with a partner to explain the terms to each other.

B. Complete each statement with one of the verbs from the following list. Underline the words that helped you to make your choice.

a. complain   b. fail   c. have   d. listen   e. lose

f. operate   g. reach   h. receive   i. send   j. use

1. People don't like to have to _____ to other people's conversations.

2. This phone costs a lot of money, so be careful and don't _____ it.

3. If the satellite systems _____, we won't be able to make a call.

4. She left me the instructions, but her system looks difficult to _____.

5. If you need to _____ me, here's the phone number where I'll be.

6. Do you _____ to be at home to get the call, or could you be at work?

7. I didn't know how much time it would take to learn to _____ this new system.

8. I finished writing, and now I'm ready to _____ you this letter.

9. I hate to _____, but this machine is not working again today.

10. If you _____ this letter, please send a reply right away.

Expanding Your Language

SPEAKING

A. Questionnaire: Use these questions to interview two people. You may want to interview people outside your class. Note their answers. Work with a partner who read a different story. Ask questions about both topics.

To carry out this activity follow these steps:

1. Practice asking and answering questions with your partner.
2. Practice introducing yourself.
3. State the topic of your questionnaire. "My questionnaire is about cell phone or e-mail use."
4. Ask for their permission to ask your questions.
5. Take turns asking your questions. Note all answers in the chart below.

Questions	Student A	Student B
1. Do you use a cell phone?		
2. Do you use e-mail?		
3. Are cell phones useful for? Give one example.		
4. What is e-mail useful for? Give one example.		
5. Can people have problems with cell phones? Give one example.		
6. Can people have problems with e-mail? Give one example.		

Work with a partner or with a small group to report on the results of your questionnaire. Share your results with your classmates.

B. Two-Minute Taped Talk: Record a 2-minute audiotape about one of the communications technologies you learned about in this chapter. To make your tape, follow the steps on page 60.

WRITING

Topic Writing—Comparing Technologies: Write about one of the technologies explained in this chapter. Write ten to fifteen sentences about how to use this tool and other sentences about the advantages and disadvantages you think are important. Use the notes you prepared and the ideas you discussed in this chapter.

To carry out this task, follow these steps:

1. Reread your notes and recall all of the information you have gathered from discussions about the advantages and disadvantages of your topic.
2. Make an outline of the information you plan to include. Refer to Chapter 3, pages 34 and 35, for an example of how to outline.
3. Check your outline against the information in the article.
4. Work with a partner who is writing on the same topic. Use your outline to explain what you plan to write. Make any changes necessary to complete your outline.
5. Do the writing and give it to your teacher.

The Internet Offers an Eye on the World

CHAPTER 15

Chapter Openers

DISCUSSION QUESTIONS

Think about these questions. Discuss your ideas with a partner or in a small group.

1. What is the Internet? How do people use the Internet today?

2. Can people talk to or see one another over the Internet?

3. What are three positive and negative points about the Internet?

Positive	Negative
a. _____	_____
b. _____	_____
c. _____	_____

4. Does the Internet help families to keep in touch with one another or keep them separated from one another? Give as many reasons as possible.

Exploring and Understanding Reading

PREDICTING

This reading is an interview with a busy young working mother whose son is in a day-care center that has Internet access so that parents can see what the children are doing during the day. From the following list, check (✓) the questions that you think the interviewer will ask. Write one question of your own.

_____ 1. Why did you choose this day-care center for your son?

_____ 2. What work do you do?

_____ 3. Are you successful in your business?

_____ 4. What does your son learn at the day-care center?

_____ 5. Is it expensive to use the Internet?

_____ 6. How often do you use the Internet to look at your son?

_____ 7. Is the Internet system safe?

8. _____

Compare your answers with a partner. Then read the interview and find out whether you predicted any of the questions.

■■

You're Only a Click Away

Today, Sally Oh is interviewing a successful executive, Amy Baines, a working mom who uses the Internet at work to watch her 3-year-old son while he is at his day care.

Sally: Tell us about your work and about Harry's schedule while you are at work.

Amy: I work at an advertising agency in New York City. I start work at 9 and finish at 6. I work all week, and sometimes I have to travel. Harry is at the day-care center from 8:30 until 6:30. It's a long day for both of us.

Sally: And you can keep in touch with Harry during the day?

Amy: That's right. I can see him whenever I want.

Sally: How do you get to see Harry during the day? The day-care center isn't near your work.

Amy: The day-care center has a video camera that is connected to a special, secure Web site. When I want to see him, I can call up the Web site on my computer and see the center on my screen.

Sally: How does that make you feel?

Amy: Wonderful. For example, when I dropped Harry off at the center yesterday, he started to cry. I had to leave, but he just wouldn't stop crying. I felt bad, but I needed to get to work. Then at work, I was so worried, I couldn't concentrate. I kept thinking about Harry. So I logged on and went to the Web site. I could see Harry playing a game, as happy as could be. It made me feel better. What a relief. I could go and concentrate on my work. I had a very productive morning.

Sally: Can anyone visit the Web site?

Amy: No. You need a special name and password to get into the system.

Sally: Do the day-care workers like it?

Amy: At first, they felt self-conscious. But now, they don't seem to notice. The activity in the day-care center goes on as usual.

Sally: How often do you log on to see your son?

Amy: It depends. Usually about four or five times a day. I just like to see him. I like to know what kind of day he's having.

Sally: Does the camera follow the children everywhere?

Amy: Almost everywhere. It's not on in the room where the children take their naps. Or in the book corner. But if I log on when he's in the book corner or if I don't see him, I ask his teacher and she brings him to a place where I can see him on camera. One time I did that so I could show him off to my boss.

Sally: Is this a good system for the day-care center to have?

Amy: I think so. It's good because I can check in and find out whether the center is doing good work with Harry. I can see for myself whether he is happy and learning and getting enough attention from the teachers. I can see whether the center is following the educational program that they say they offer. I like what I see (there is a variety of interesting activities, and all of the children get individual attention), and so I recommended the center to two friends who were looking for good day care for their kids.

Sally: Are there any other benefits to this system?

Amy: Yes. My parents, who live 2,000 miles away, can log on and see their first grandchild learning to do all of those milestone activities: reading and writing for the first time. One time, for example, my father logged on and Harry wrote, "Hi, Grandpa" and held it up to the screen. My father was so happy. He wrote me an e-mail right away. With the Internet, it's as though we're living in the same house.

UNDERSTANDING DETAILS

Answer the following questions. In the interview, underline the parts that support your answer. Mark the question number in the margin.

1. What is Amy's work schedule?

   _____

   _____

2. What is Harry's day-care schedule?

   _____

   _____

3. When can Amy see Harry at day care? How does she do this?

   _____

   _____

4. How does this make Amy feel? Give an example.

   _____

   _____

5. Do the day-care workers like the system?

   _____

   _____

6. How often does Amy look at her son during the day?

   _____

   _____

7. What does Amy think of the quality of education at the center? Give three facts to support your answer.

   _____

   _____

Work with a partner. Read your questions and answers. Refer to the reading if you have different answers.

UNDERSTANDING EXAMPLES

In the interview, Amy gives two examples to explain why the Internet service is good for her and Harry. In the reading, locate the information given for these explanations. Write the important details in note form.

Why Amy Likes Harry's Online Day Care

Example 1: Checking on Harry at day care after she dropped him off	**Example 2:** Grandparents log on
What happened:	**What happened:**
1st:	1st:
2nd:	2nd:
3rd:	3rd:
Feelings:	Feelings:

Work with a partner. Take turns using your notes to tell back these examples.

After Reading

APPLYING THE INFORMATION: PROBLEM SOLVING

Your school is thinking of offering an e-class: a course that you follow via the Internet with an e-mail address and video hookup so that students can "attend" their class and exchange communication with the teacher and other students while at home. A group of people wants you to make a presentation showing the benefits of this idea and listing the questions about this type of course that people may have.

To do this, follow these steps:

1. Make a list of three possible benefits and questions. Use some of the ideas and questions from the interview to help you make this list. Work with a partner to compare your ideas.
2. Together, develop a list of three or more benefits. Prepare some examples to support your case.
3. Make a list of three questions you have about this new Internet class.
4. Share these ideas with others in a small group. Decide on a common list of benefits and questions.
5. Report on your list to the class.

Vocabulary Building

VOCABULARY IN CONTEXT

A. Complete each sentence with one of the words from the following list. Underline the words that helped you choose your answer.

a. concentrate   b. connect   c. notice   d. offer

e. password   f. productive   g. recommend

h. self-conscious

1. Can you _____ me to the people who produced this program so that I can ask them some questions?

2. I asked her to tell me the special _____ so that I could get into the program and get the file I needed.

3. Your work is excellent. I would be happy to _____ you for the job.

4. She was happy that they could _____ her the job she wanted.

5. I was nervous and felt very _____ about the people who were watching me.

6. I was worried and so it was difficult to _____ on finishing my work.

7. I finished all of my work after lunch. It was a very

   _____ afternoon.

8. I was watching TV, so I didn't _____ how late it was.

Check your answers. Work with a partner and take turns reading the completed sentences.

In English, writers use examples to explain a general idea in detail. Usually, these sentences follow the statement of the idea. There are different ways to show the reader that the writer is explaining by example. Many writers use the words *such as*, *like*, *for example*, or *for instance* to introduce the examples.

B. Matching Ideas and Examples: Match the sentence in Column A with the example in Column B that fits it best.

Column A

Column B

_____ 1. My father can log on and look at what Harry is doing.

a. I did some research to find out whether the service has safety precautions, for example, a special password and a secure Web site.

_____ 2. Can you see him any time of the day?

b. For example, during the week, I usually get up at 6:00 A.M., and I don't stop until about 7:00 P.M.

_____ 3. I wanted to know whether they had a good program.

c. For example, did they offer special programs, such as art and reading?

_____ 4. How do you know whether the service is safe?

d. For instance, one day, he watched Harry writing for the first time.

_____ 5. I lead a very busy life most of the time.

e. Yes. One day, for example, I logged on at 7 in the morning.

Check your answers. Work with a partner to take turns reading the pairs that match.

Expanding Your Language

Discussion Questions: Look at this graph and then think about the following questions. Share your ideas with a partner or in a small group.

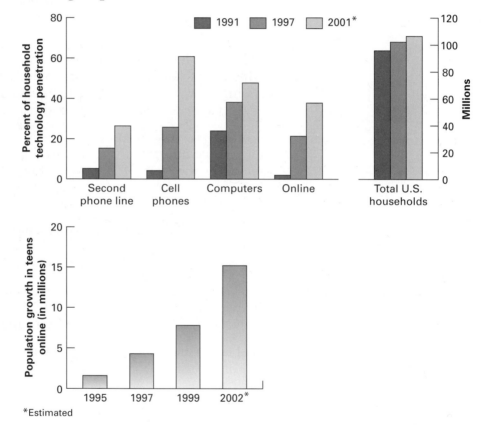

*Estimated

1. How popular is household technology becoming for Americans? What effect could this have on people?

2. Why is the Internet attracting teenagers? What are the benefits and dangers?

QUESTIONNAIRE: USING THE INTERNET

Answer these questions for yourself and add a question of your own. Ask two classmates these same questions.

Questions	You	Student A	Student B
1. Do/did you ever use the Internet?			
2. What are some useful things you can do on the Internet?			
3. What are some disadvantage to using the Internet?			
4. In the future, how will people use the Internet?			
5.			

Work with a partner or in a small group. Take turns telling each other about the information you received. Share the information with others in your class.

WRITING

Topic Writing: From the information in the chapter readings, discussions, and the questionnaire, make a list of three advantages and disadvantages of the Internet. Try to include one example for each of the ideas on your list.

Work with a group to share the ideas on your lists. Add any ideas you can to your list. Use your list to make an outline to write from. To do this, follow the steps on pages 34 and 35.

Read On: Taking It Further

READING CLOZE

■ **READINGTIP:** *Don't forget to write your reading journal and vocabulary log entries in your notebook. Show the entries to your teacher. Arrange to discuss your progress in reading.*

Use words listed here from the unit to fill in the blanks in this paragraph.

a. buy   b. communicate   c. gather   d. make   e. meet

f. rent   g. receive   h. research   i. talk   j. write

More and more people use the Internet. They (1) _____ online for many different reasons. Some people want to

(2)_____ things electronically instead of going out shopping. People are using the Internet to arrange their travel. They buy

tickets and (3)_____ arrangements for hotels, entertainment, and even reservations for dinner. Travelers can

(4)_____ cars over the Internet. Some schools use the

Internet for (5)_____. Students are able to

(6)_____ information electronically. They can

(7)_____ with people in faraway places. People of all

ages (8)_____ other people who share their interests and

(9)_____ messages to them. They send these messages

by e-mail, and then they (10)_____ answers from people they have never met.

Check your answers.

NEWSPAPER ARTICLES

Every day there are new developments in technology. Ask your teacher for a short newspaper article that you can read. Choose an article about a recent development in technology discussed in this unit, such as cell phones or the Internet. Read the article over until you have a good idea of the important facts of the story. Explain your article to a partner or in a small group.

WORD PLAY: A NEW-FASHIONED SPELLING BEE

Work in small groups of four or more. Form two teams within each group. Each team makes a list of ten to fifteen (or more!) important vocabulary words in this unit. Check to make sure that you have the correct spelling. You can assign certain parts of the alphabet to avoid having words appear on both lists. Teams take turns asking the other team to spell a word on its list. The team to spell the most words correctly wins. You can make the game more difficult by varying the rules. Suggestions include using the word correctly in a sentence, spelling without writing, or spelling within a time limit.

UNIT 6

Leisure

Time flies.
– English Proverb

Introducing the Topics

Leisure time is that time of the day, week, month, or year when we can do the things we enjoy or when we have time to ourselves. This unit examines the idea of leisure time in the United States today. Chapter 16 asks questions about what's happened to leisure time in today's society. How does leisure time today compare to that in the past? In Chapter 17, we compare two competing leisure activities: going out to the movies and staying home with a video. Which do we prefer? Chapter 18 looks into a popular U.S. destination: the mall. What kinds of attractions do today's malls offer?

Points of Interest

What kinds of leisure activities do you think are popular today?

CHAPTER 16

Today's Workweek: Do We Need Time Out?

Chapter Openers

DISCUSSION QUESTIONS: LEISURE TIME

Think about these questions. Discuss your ideas with a partner or in a small group.

1. How much leisure time do you have
   a. every day?
   b. during the week?
   c. during the year?

2. What kinds of leisure activities do you enjoy?

3. a. How much leisure time do you think you need?
   b. Do you feel that you're getting enough time, not enough, or too much?
   c. What would you do if you had more free time?

4. Do you think that people have more leisure time today than they did 30, 50, or 100 years ago? Give reasons for your answers.

GETTING INFORMATION FROM A GRAPH

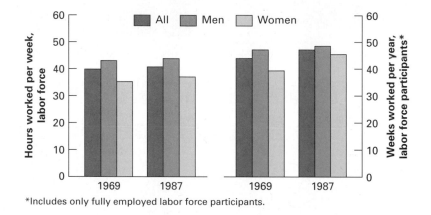

*Includes only fully employed labor force participants.

Discuss this question with a partner: Why do you think we have less leisure time today than in the past?

Exploring and Understanding Reading

PREDICTING: AGREE/DISAGREE

Write *A* if you agree or *D* if you disagree with the statement.

———— 1. In the future, people will work fewer hours at their jobs.

———— 2. People today need to work longer hours or to find a second job in order to pay their bills.

———— 3. Companies are trying to save money, and so people are losing their jobs.

———— 4. New communications technology, such as e-mail and cell phones, gives us more free time.

———— 5. When people go on vacation, they don't bring work with them or keep in touch with their offices.

Work with a partner. Compare your answers. You don't have to agree, but explain your reasons as completely as possible. After you finish reading, return to these questions and answer them, based on the information you read.

PREVIEWING

To preview, read the title and the first and last sentences of each paragraph in the reading. Make a list of three ideas you expect to find out about in this reading. The first idea is done as an example.

1. *Today, people are working many hours more than in the past.*

2. _____

3. _____

Compare your choices with a partner. Try to agree on your answers.

Read the complete article. Return to the list and change or add to your answers.

■ ■
_____

The Growth of Work

A.   In the future, people will work fewer hours a week, right? Actually, today, more people are working 10 to 12 hours a day, 6 days a week, than ever before in this century. People put in the same hours as workers in the 1860–1870s did in the days before there were labor unions. In the 1950s, most people worked a 40-hour workweek. At that time, people predicted that the workweek would continue to decrease to 30 hours or less. Sociologists asked, "What will people do with all their free time?" Today, people are asking, "When will I get some free time?"

B.   More people are working longer hours, for two reasons. One reason is the increase in the cost of living. In order to support a family today, people have to work longer hours or work at a second job. Take the example of Lily P. She works in New Jersey as a social worker from 8:30 until 2:30 P.M. In the late afternoon and in the evenings, she sees private clients in her home office. On the weekends, she works as a caterer. She makes specialty cakes for weddings, anniversaries, and birthdays and delivers them to her customers. In one week, she earns about $950 to support herself and her two children. According to Lily, who is a single mother, she has to keep working the hours she does. It costs so much to support her family, she says, that working less is not possible. But there is a second reason that people are working more than 40 hours a week. Today, many companies are trying to do more work with fewer workers. These companies have reduced the number of employees in order to save money and to make higher profits. But they need to stay competitive, so they ask their employees to work longer hours. Employees feel that they have no choice. If they don't work overtime, they are afraid that they will be fired.

C.   Changes in technology make it easier for people to be working all the time, even when they are on vacation or when they are with their families at home. People who work on personal computers are taking their work home with them on weekends and in the evenings. Elaine G. works for an insurance company. She works a flexible schedule so that she can be with her nine-month-old baby. She spends 24 hours a week at the office. Then she is supposed to work another 16 hours on her computer at home. She hoped that she could have more time to be with her baby. But she works more than 16 hours at home to complete her work. She says, "My boss just wants the job done. If I don't finish the work, he thinks I'm not really working at home." With faxes, cell phones, and e-mail, people can work even when they are on vacation. About 30 percent of people who answered one poll said that they checked their voice mail or answering machines once during their vacation. Some people even check their voice or e-mail once a day.

D.   Where will technology and the demands of the workweek take us? If things continue this way into the future, we may never get to leave the office, at least not for long. Or people may begin to say, "This is enough. I need my leisure time."

_____

UNDERSTANDING DETAILS

A. Complete the statement, based on the information in the reading. In the reading, underline the words that support your answer.

■ *READING TIP:*
Remember to use the words of the question to help you look quickly and locate the answer.

1. Today, people are working _____ they did in the 1860s.

2. In the 1950s, people predicted that the workweek would

_____ .

3. Today, people are asking

_____ .

4. In order to support a family today,

_____ .

5. Today, many companies are trying to

_____ .

6. People who work on personal computers are

_____ .

7. About 30 percent of people who answered one poll said

_____ .

B. Answer the following questions. In the reading, mark the question number in the margin where you found the information for your answer.

1. What are the two reasons that people are working longer hours today?

    a. _____

    b. _____

2. Why does Lily say that she has to work long hours? Which of the two reasons in question 1 relates to her situation?

    _____

    _____

3. Why does Elaine say that she has to work long hours at home? Which of the two reasons in question 1 relates to her situation?

    _____

    _____

4. With new technology, when can people work today?

    a. _____

    b. _____

5. Why does Elaine say that she has to put in more hours to finish her work at home?

_____

_____

6. What are two possibilities for working hours in the future?

a. _____

b. _____

Work with a partner. Read your questions and answers. Refer to the reading if you have different answers.

UNDERSTANDING EXAMPLES

In this article, we learn about the stories of two people, Lily and Elaine. They are women who are working long hours. Their experiences are examples of a general situation among many workers today.

Locate the information given for these examples in the reading. In note form, write the important details of their stories.

	Lily: Supporting the Family	*Elaine: Keeping the Job*
Profile:		
Work they do:		
Personal background:		
Reasons for working long hours:		

Work with a partner. Take turns using your notes to explain these examples.

After Reading

QUESTIONNAIRE: Work Time/Free Time

Ask two people who are working to answer these questions. Note their answers.

Questions	Person A	Person B
1. Where do you work?		
2. What job do you do?		
3. How much time do you spend working?		
4. How much free time do you have?		
5. What do you do in your free time?		
6. In the future, would you like to have more free time? Explain your reasons.		

Work with a partner or others in a small group. Report the answers to each other. Be prepared to present your results to the class.

GIVING YOUR OPINION

Based on the reading, the questionnaire reports, and your own ideas, answer the following questions.

1. Will people have more or less free time in the future? Give some reasons for your opinion.

2. How much free time would you like to have in the future?

3. What kinds of leisure activities do you think that people would like to do in the future?

Discuss your ideas with a partner or in a small group.

Vocabulary Building

VOCABULARY IN CONTEXT

A. Complete each sentence with one of the nouns from the list. Underline the words that helped you make your choice.

a. client   b. demands   c. employees   d. increase

e. reasons   f. schedule   g. vacation

1. She worked late so that she could meet and talk to a

    _____ who had an important problem to solve.

2. The company asked whether any of its _____ could stay late and work extra hours to finish the job.

3. There has been an _____ in the number of people who work a flexible schedule.

4. Everyone needs to relax and take a _____ at least once a year.

5. The workers had a list of _____ for improvement that they wanted the company to listen to.

6. I forgot my _____, so I didn't know what time I had to start work.

7. There are probably many _____ why people are working longer hours today.

B. Complete each sentence with one of the verbs from the following list. Underline the words that helped you to make your choice.

a. check   b. complete   c. continue   d. deliver

e. hope   f. reduce   g. support

1. Can you _____ this food in time for the party tonight?

2. How long can you _____ to work without taking a break?

3. Would you please _____ the voice mail and see whether we've heard from that customer today?

4. They _____ the work will be finished by tomorrow night.

5. He needs enough money to be able to pay his bills and

   _____ himself.

6. Did you _____ all the work that I left for you this morning?

7. The company is in trouble, and it will have to _____ the number of workers on the night shift.

Check your answers. Take turns reading the sentences.

ANTONYMS

Match the word in Column A with its antonym in Column B.

Column A   **Column B**

_____ 1. fewer   a. arrive

_____ 2. reduce   b. question

_____ 3. answer   c. work

_____ 4. longer   d. more

_____ 5. easier   e. harder

_____ 6. leisure   f. impossible

_____ 7. leave   g. inflexible

_____ 8. complete   h. increase

_____ 9. possible   i. shorter

_____ 10. flexible   j. incomplete

In English, certain prefixes, such as *il-*, *im-*, *un-*, *in-*, and others, are added to the beginning of an adjective to give the word its antonym, or opposite meaning.

Underline four words from the list that have an antonym that begins with one of these negative prefixes. Think of more words like these that you know.

Expanding Your Language

READING FROM THE NEWS: ASKING INFORMATION QUESTIONS

Choose story A, which follows, or story B, which is in the Exercise Pages section of the book. Student A works with the story that follows. Student B works with story B, which is in the exercise on page E-5. Complete the following steps for both stories:

1. Read the information questions about your story.
2. Read to find out the main idea of the story.
3. Underline the important facts that give the answers to the questions.
4. To compare the facts you underlined, work with a partner who read the same story.
5. Take turns asking and answering each other's questions.
6. Write the answers in note form.
7. Use your notes and take turns explaining as much of the story as you can.

Information Questions

1. What kind of vacation is this?

2. What kind of people go on this type of vacation?

3. How expensive it is?

4. What are the attractions of this kind of vacation?

5. What are the disadvantages?

RETELLING THE STORY

1. Work with a partner who read story B. Explain your story to each other. Ask and answer each other's questions.

2. Use the questions and answers to help you write about one of the stories.

3. Choose a short newspaper article, like the story you read, from your local paper. Make a copy of the article and work with a partner. Follow the steps in "Reading from the News" and step 1 of "Retelling the Story" to prepare to discuss your article.

Story A: Taking a Trip in the Car

Many ordinary Americans love to drive when they take a vacation. When Americans take trips for pleasure, they usually take their own cars. For most long-distance trips, Americans travel across more than one state; in fact, more than 60 percent of long-distance trips were interstate trips. Statistics show that men drive more often than women do. Most of the car-driving vacationers were of middle-class background. A majority had had a university education. Why do they like to drive? There are many practical reasons, such as saving money, but most say that they like the sense of control and freedom they get by being behind the wheel. People's greatest worry was that they might have car trouble on the road.

CHAPTER

Entertainment Choices

Chapter Openers

CATEGORIZING

Read the following statements. Write *V* if they refer to watching videos at home, *M* if they describe going out to the movies, or *B* if they can describe both.

_____ 1. I can watch any movie I want to.

_____ 2. I can enjoy the movie with lots of other people.

_____ 3. I can see the action on a big screen.

_____ 4. I can see three for the price of one.

_____ 5. I can watch any time I want.

Discuss your answers with a partner.

PAIRED READINGS

Here are two personal essays written to show why the writers like the things they do. Choose one of the essays and find out the advantages and disadvantages of going out to the movies or staying home with the television.

■■

Reading 1: At Home with the TV

LISTING ADVANTAGES

What are some of the reasons people stay home to watch television? List three positive reasons for spending time watching television.

1. _____

2. _____

3. _____

Discuss your ideas with a partner or in a small group.

UNDERSTANDING THE MAIN IDEAS

Read both of the paragraphs in this reading. Write a sentence that expresses the main idea of each paragraph.

A. _____

B. _____

UNDERSTANDING DETAILS

Answer the questions after each paragraph. Underline the facts that support your answer. Write the question number in the margin of the reading.

Confessions of a Couch Potato

A.   I have a confession to make. My idea of a perfect evening is to stay at home, eat in, and watch TV. There are so many good shows on these days. And there are so many new channels. I could watch television all night. There's broadcasting 24 hours a day. First, I'll catch the news. With cable, I get two 24 hour news stations. There's even a station that shows the news every 15 minutes. Some nights, I'll watch a news documentary. There's a documentary shown every night of the week on at least one channel. Then there're the sit-coms. The funny ones are on early in the evening. The dramatic shows are on later. After that there's the late-night news and, of course, late-night talk shows. Of course, that's just during the week. On the weekends, I don't watch TV: well, not exactly.

---

1. What is the author's idea of a perfect evening?

   _____

   _____

2. How many hours of broadcasting can this person watch?

   _____

   _____

3. How many 24-hour news channels are there?

   _____

   _____

4. How often can this person watch the news?

   _____

   _____

5. What are three other kinds of programs this person likes to watch?

   a. _____

   b. _____

   c. _____

6. Does this person watch TV on the weekend?

   _____

   _____

B.   On the weekends, I go to my video store and get a few good movies to watch on my VCR. I would rather watch a movie at home than go out. It costs less and I can really get comfortable. I can pause the video when I want to get up and get something to eat. I'm not exactly a couch potato. That's because I don't watch television in the living room, where my couch is. My television is in my bedroom. So I can watch while I'm in bed. I know it's not a good habit, but insomnia is not something I worry about. Maybe I should worry about watching so much TV.

1. What does the author do on the weekends?

   _____

   _____

2. Why would the author rather watch a movie at home?

   _____

   _____

3. Why isn't this person a couch potato?

   _____

   _____

4. Where does the author watch TV?

   _____

   _____

5. a. What does the author not worry about?

   _____

   b. What should the author worry about?

   _____

Work with a partner. Take turns reading the questions and answers. Refer to the information in the reading if you have different answers.

RECAPPING THE INFORMATION

Work with a partner who read the same story. Together, underline the important facts in both paragraphs. Then use the information to complete a note-taking chart:

The Perfect Night In:

- *stay at home*
- *eat in*
- *watch TV*

Programs I Like to Watch:

Practice telling the information to your partner. Try not to read the notes as you speak. Ask for help if you forget or give incorrect information. Ask your partner to retell the information.

REACTING TO THE INFORMATION

Make a list of three or four reasons for and against staying home to watch TV. Use information from the reading and ideas of your own. Write your ideas in note form, as shown in italic in the following chart.

Advantages	*Disadvantages*
1. *Be comfortable at home*	*Not getting physical exercise*
2.	
3.	
4.	

Work with a partner and share your ideas. Together, make a list of your best ideas to share with others.

Discuss this question with others: Is staying home to watch television a good idea? Why or why not?

■ ■
_____

Reading 2: Out at the Movies

LISTING ADVANTAGES

What are some of the reasons people like to go out to the movies? List three positive reasons for choosing to see a movie in a theater.

1. _____

2. _____

3. _____

Discuss your ideas with a partner or in a small group.

UNDERSTANDING THE MAIN IDEAS

Read both of the paragraphs that follow. Write a sentence that expresses the main idea of each paragraph.

A. _____

B. _____

UNDERSTANDING DETAILS

Answer the questions after each paragraph. Underline the facts that support your answer. Write the question number in the margin of the reading.

Confessions of a Movie Fan

A.   On a cold winter night, I know that there are lots of reasons to stay home and watch videos, but I love to go out to the movies. The films look better in the theater. The screen is so wide that it seems to surround you. You really get the feeling that you are closer to the action. The costumes and the settings look so much more beautiful on the big screen. And, of course, because of the equipment and the acoustics in the theater, the sound is so much better, too. The special effects don't look or sound as good at home. Plus, I like seeing a movie with other people in the theater. The reaction of the crowd can intensify my feelings. I like noticing the parts of the movie people laugh at or cry over. I like listening to the reaction of people after the movie is over. I even like watching the previews and the special messages before the movie starts. The previews can be really funny, and they help me to decide whether I want to see the film when it comes out. Last, but not least, I love the popcorn.

1. What does the author love to do?

   _____

   _____

2. Why is the sound better at the movies?

   _____

   _____

3. How does seeing special effects at the movies compare to seeing them at home?

   _____

   _____

4. Why does the author like seeing movies with other people at the theater?

   _____

   _____

5. Why does the author like the previews?

   _____

   _____

B.   Seeing a movie is a social event. I enjoy going out and making an evening out of it. If I'm with a friend, we'll go and have coffee either before or after the film. It's really my idea of a good date. If there's a film I especially like, I'll invite someone out and see it again. If the film is very moving or extremely well done, I might go back two or three times. If I'm alone, I usually go during the week when the ticket price is lower. On the week-end, the tickets are more expensive and the lines are very long. I like going with friends to repertoire theaters. You can see some of the old classics or movies by a well-known director. The theater gives a special student rate, so we don't have to pay much to go. In some cities, there are film festivals that show new and experimental films. At the festival, there are a lot of people who come to see these films. There is often a lot of excitement at these events

_____

1. What does the author enjoy doing?

_____

_____

2. Where does the author like to go before or after a film?

_____

_____

3. How many times does the author like to go to see a movie?

_____

_____

4. Why is it better to go to a film during the week?

_____

_____

5. What other kind of films does the author like to see?

_____

_____

Work with a partner. Take turns reading the questions and answers. Refer to the information in the reading if you have different answers.

RECAPPING THE INFORMATION

Work with a partner who read the same information. Together, underline the important facts in both paragraphs. Then use the information to complete a note-taking chart:

The Perfect Night Out:

- *go to the movies—even if it's cold*

Reasons I Prefer Movies:

- *films look better on wide screen; feel you are there*
- *beautiful costumes*

Practice telling the information to your partner. Try not to read the notes as you speak. Ask for help if you forget or give incorrect information. Ask your partner to retell the information.

REACTING TO THE INFORMATION

Make a list of three or four reasons for and against going out to the movies. Use information from the reading and ideas of your own. Write your ideas in note form, as shown in the following chart.

Advantages	Disadvantages
1. *Enjoyment of seeing images on the large screen*	*Waiting in long lines*
2.	
3.	
4.	

Work with a partner and share your ideas. Together, make a list of your best ideas to share with others.

Discuss this question with others: What are the reasons you like going out to the movies?

Vocabulary Building

MATCHING MEANINGS

For each word in Column A, write the letter of the word in Column B that has the opposite meaning.

Column A	Column B
_____ 1. overlooked	a. arrived
_____ 2. laugh	b. narrow
_____ 3. special	c. slowly
_____ 4. get up	d. appreciated
_____ 5. quickly	e. never
_____ 6. left	f. ordinary
_____ 7. always	g. finish
_____ 8. start	h. cry
_____ 9. wide	i. sit down

Check your answers. Write three or more sentences, using at least two of the words from the lists in each sentence.

CATEGORIZING

Circle the word or phrase that does not belong in each of these groups. Tell why it doesn't belong there.

1. 24 hours   station   evening   late night   weekend

2. dramatic   documentary   sitcoms   news programs   channels

3. costume   settings   acoustics   special effects   previews

4. video store   bed   living room   couch   bedroom

5. usually   quickly   interesting   really   very

Expanding Your Language

SPEAKING

Movie or Video Review: Work with a partner or in a small group. Choose a movie or a video that everyone in the group can agree they would like to see together. Together, prepare to talk about the important elements of the film you will see. Include the following information:

Movie/Video Survey

Name of the movie: _____

1. What kind of movie is it?

   - comedy
   - romance
   - action
   - drama
   - science fiction
   - biography
   - history

2. Who are the main characters?

3. What are the main parts of the story, or plot of the film?

4. Where and when does the movie take place?

5. Would you tell other people to see this movie? Why or why not?

A. After the movie, get together with others and complete the form. Practice explaining about the film to each other.

B. Get together with a partner who saw a different film and talk about the film you saw.

WRITING

Use the notes you prepared for your movie survey to write about the film you saw.

CHAPTER 18

Meeting at the Mall: America's Growing Leisure Activity

Chapter Openers

DISCUSSION QUESTIONS

Think about these questions. Share your ideas with a partner or in a small group.

1. Why are shopping malls popular?

2. Compare: How are shopping malls in other countries similar to or different from those in the United States?

MATCHING

Match each of these activities to the correct illustration. Check (✔) the activities that you think people go to malls to do. Think of as much information to give to explain your choices.

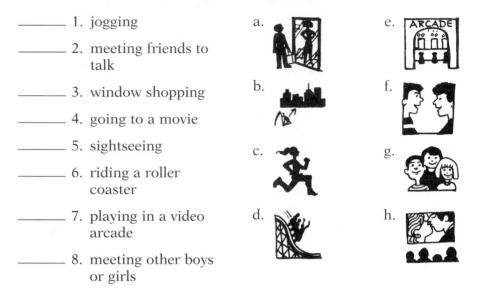

_____ 1. jogging

_____ 2. meeting friends to talk

_____ 3. window shopping

_____ 4. going to a movie

_____ 5. sightseeing

_____ 6. riding a roller coaster

_____ 7. playing in a video arcade

_____ 8. meeting other boys or girls

Exploring and Understanding Reading

PREVIEWING

In English, writers often state the main idea in the first one or two sentences of the paragraph. Read the beginning sentences of each paragraph. Write the letter of the paragraph that best fits each of these main idea statements.

_____ 1. the interest tourists have in visiting malls in the United States

_____ 2. the many activities local people can do at the mall

_____ 3. the increasing interest in visiting malls in the United States

_____ 4. the good and bad effects of malls on the economy

Compare your answers with a partner. Read the whole article and confirm your answers.

It's a Mall World After All

A.   What is the favorite destination in the United Sates? It's not a national park or the Statue of Liberty. It's the mall. Malls are attracting more and more people. Malls were designed for people to get all of their shopping done conveniently. Malls used to be called "shopping centers." But today, people who are heading for the malls have more than shopping in mind. In fact, for some people, shopping is the last thing they're thinking of.

B.   There are more than 300 malls in the United States, and the largest contain more than 200 different shops. The Mall of America in Bloomington, Minnesota, is one of the country's largest malls. It has more than 400 stores, 50 restaurants, 9 nightclubs, and a roller-coaster. In 1995, about 40 million people visited this huge shopping center. Some of the visitors were tourists. People visiting from overseas want to buy presents to bring home to families and friends. But that is not the only reason they come. Some tourists want to experience what they describe as "consumer heaven." One young man from France expressed his feelings this way: "Now that we've seen the sights at the mall, we can go home." Some people plan their vacations around their shopping plans. Some malls are planning big entertainment centers to add to their appeal. In Washington, more people visit the Potomac Mills shopping center than visit Mount Vernon or Arlington National Cemetery. Potomac Mills attracts about 660,000 international shoppers and 23 million domestic shoppers each year.

C.   Large malls attract tourists, but the small malls in cities and towns throughout the country are attractive to locals, especially to teens and seniors. Why do these people come to the mall? Malls are becoming popular spots for older people to get together for their morning exercise. Jack Donner and his wife, Margo, meet up at 7:00 A.M. with six friends in their seventies for a 10-mile daily hike. They wear running shoes and jogging outfits and walk at a fast pace through the mall. By 8:30 they are ready for a break and breakfast at their favorite café, which is in the mall. According to Jack, the mall suits their needs perfectly. It's a safe place, it's protected from the weather, it's quiet, and, at 7:00 A.M., not crowded. Shopping is secondary; the mall's a good place to socialize. Socializing is also on the minds of teenagers, who come to the malls after school and on the weekends. Kids meet their friends to talk. They walk around and look at what's on sale, but they don't spend a lot of money on shopping. They spend most of the afternoon sitting on the benches outside the food courts, just hanging out with their friends.

D.   Some people say that malls are good for the economy. They provide jobs and taxes for the government. But others criticize the traffic jams, the crowds, and the low-paying jobs that are available to most of the people who work there. Environmentalists complain that the builders and developers are destroying good farm and forest land when they put up these large malls. Some people say that malls take business away from small stores and local family businesses. Some parents say that they don't like their kids to spend their free time sitting around talking and looking at things to buy. But others like the convenience of malls, and they like paying lower prices at the big discount stores found there. Malls may not appeal to everyone, but throughout the United States, they are a favorite destination for many.

UNDERSTANDING DETAILS

In note form, write the answers to the questions. In the reading, underline the words that support your answers. Write the question number in the margin.

1. What is America's favorite destination?

   _____

   _____

2. a. How many malls are there in the United States?

      _____

   b. What do the largest contain?

      _____

3. List these important details about the Mall of America:

   a. Location: _____

   b. Number of stores: _____

   c. Number of restaurants: _____

   d. Number of nightclubs: _____

   e. Visitors: _____

4. What are two reasons that tourists visit the mall?

   a. _____

   b. _____

5. What three details show that U.S. malls are popular with tourists?

   a. _____

   b. _____

   c. _____

6. What two groups of people like visiting malls near their homes?

   a. _____

   b. _____

LISTING FACTS

1. List these important details about activities in the malls:

	Group A	Group B
Activity:	_____	_____
When:	_____	_____
How long:	_____	_____
Advantages:	_____	_____

2. What do people say about the effect of malls on the economy?

   a. Positive effects: _____

   b. Negative effects: _____

Work with a partner. Read your questions and answers. Refer to the reading if you have different answers.

After Reading

WHO SAID THAT?

Read and identify the speaker for each of the statements, based on the information in the reading. Write *T* for tourist, *S* for senior, and *TE* for teenager.

_____ 1. One of the things I most wanted to do while I was here was to visit this mall. I just couldn't go home without getting presents for people back home.

_____ 2. She told me that she'd meet me here right after school. It's almost 5 o'clock. I'm going to have to get home soon, but I've got to talk to her.

_____ 3. Come with me and look at this dress. I don't have enough for it, but it would look great on you.

_____ 4. Come and join us tomorrow morning. Wear something comfortable, and meet us in front of Little Jack's at 7:00.

_____ 5. The guard told us we had to leave. We can't sit in the food court after 11:30 P.M.

_____ 6. This is the most amazing place. I saw it advertised at the travel bureau, but I really couldn't imagine how big and crowded it would be. There's so much here; I could spend the whole day walking around.

_____ 7. Judy told me that there's this really good-looking boy who is always here with his friends.

Work with a partner. Take turns reading and then identifying whose statements these could be.

EVALUATING THE INFORMATION: READING FROM THE NEWS

Read the short article that follows, and then discuss these questions.

1. What are some churches doing?

2. Why are they doing this?

3. Where is the Anglican Church located?

4. What are some of the feelings, both positive and negative, that people have about this new church location?

■ ■
_____

Churches in Malls Give New Meaning to Sunday Shopping

Some churches are now holding services in retail malls as an added attraction to one-stop Sunday shopping. The move is aimed at bringing new members to churches that are in financial trouble. According to Paul MacLean, a consultant for the Anglican Church of Canada, "Malls are the great collecting points of people in our culture now." The church is out in the marketplace, along with clothing stores, fast-food joints, and all of that. According to the Anglican Church, it has been a mixed success. Malls are attracting a lot of people. There's a lot of energy. But there's a problem. It doesn't feel like a church to some people.

What's your opinion? Are malls a good location for religious services?

_____

Vocabulary Building

VOCABULARY IN CONTEXT

Use a word from the following list to complete the sentences. Underline the words that helped you to choose your answers.

a. attract   b. contain   c. criticize   d. describe

e. experience   f. express   g. meet   h. provide

i. socialize   j. spend

1. They want to _____ how it feels to live in another country.

2. They often _____ their friends at the mall for coffee and conversation.

3. The new store will _____ jobs for many people in the area.

4. I have no more money to _____ on new clothes this month.

5. I found three birthday cards with messages that _____ my feelings exactly.

6. They put up beautiful new signs to _____ customers to their stores.

7. Can you _____ what the new shopping center looks like?

8. I don't like to _____, but this food tastes terrible.

9. These boxes _____ all the parts you'll need to finish the project.

10. This place is so popular that everyone goes there to _____.

Check your answers. Work with a partner and take turns reading the sentences.

WORD FORM

Decide whether the word in boldface is a noun *(N)* or a verb *(V)*. Then write five sentences of your own, showing how to use the word in boldface as a different part of speech.

_____ 1. We decided to go to the gym and **exercise** after work.

_____ 2. A nice long **walk** will be good for you.

_____ 3. I think the **pace** of life today is too slow.

_____ 4. I liked the **design** of the old building better than the new.

_____ 5. Visiting the old city was the best **experience** of the trip.

_____ 6. She decided to organize the **visit** for a time when we could be together.

_____ 7. They got together to **plan** the surprise birthday party.

Check your answers. Work with a partner and take turns reading the sentences.

▮ Expanding Your Language

WRITING

Topic Writing: Write a paragraph about the advantages and disadvantages of malls. Write some sentences about the advantages and others about the disadvantages. Use the information you read about in this chapter and any ideas of your own.

To carry out this task, follow these steps:

1. Reread the articles in this chapter and brainstorm a list of good and bad points about malls. Discuss these ideas with others in a small group. Try to add ideas to your list.
2. Make an outline of the information you plan to include. Refer to Chapter 3, pages 34–35, for an example of how to outline.
3. Work with a partner. Use your outline to explain what you plan to write. Make any changes necessary to complete your outline.
4. Write the paragraph.
5. Work with a partner and explain to each other the ideas you wrote about.
6. Give the paragraph to your teacher.

SPEAKING

You read that malls are a tourist attraction in the United States. What is your idea of a good place to visit when you are on vacation?

Look at the following graph. Based on the information in the graph, answer the following questions. Work with a partner or a small group to discuss your answers.

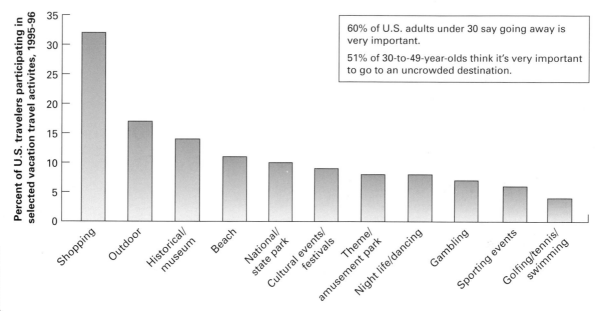

> 60% of U.S. adults under 30 say going away is very important.
>
> 51% of 30-to-49-year-olds think it's very important to go to an uncrowded destination.

1. What is the favorite activity of Americans on vacation?

   _____

   _____

2. What do 60 percent of Americans under thirty think about vacations?

   _____

   _____

3. What do 51 percent of Americans ages thirty to forty-nine think about vacations?

   _____

   _____

Questionnaire

Answer these questions for yourself. Ask two others the same questions.

Questions	You	Student A	Student B
1. Where would you like to go on vacation?			
2. What would you like to do on vacation? • read • play sports • travel • visit friends and family • go shopping			
3. How often would you like to take a vacation?			
4. How long would you like to spend on vacation?			
5. Who would you like to go on vacation with? • family member • friend • alone			

Work with a partner. Take turns explaining the information you gathered. Share your information with others in the class.

▮ **Read On: Taking It Further**

READING CLOZE

▪ *READING TIP: Look over your reading journal and vocabulary log entries. Look over the reading work you have done in this book. Prepare to discuss this question: How has my reading improved?*

Use words listed here from the unit to fill in the blanks in this paragraph.

a. arrange   b. carry   c. check   d. forget   e. keep

f. never   g. possible   h. provide   i. travel   j. work

Usually, American workers get 2 weeks of vacation a year. But

today, more Americans are taking (1) _____ with them when they go on vacation. With today's technology, a person

can (2) _____ to another country and still

(3) _____ in touch with the home office. With cell

phones and e-mail, the office is (4) _____ far away.

Many people (5) _____ their e-mail during their

vacation. People (6) _____ their cell phones on the

beach. Many tour companies (7) _____ to have Internet

access for their clients on cruise ships. Hotels (8) _____ computers for their guests. Some people say that this technology

makes it (9) _____ to go on vacation. Other people say that when they go on vacation, they want to be able to

(10) _____ about work.

Check your answers.

NEWSPAPER ARTICLES

Check the newspaper for articles about leisure and leisure activities like those you read about in this unit. Ask your teacher for short articles that you can read. One suggestion is to look for articles about places to visit and things to do that you can find in the travel or entertainment sections of the newspaper. Read the article over until you have a good idea of the important facts of the story. Explain your article to a partner or in a small group.

WORD PLAY

Choose one of the word-play activities described in the "Read On" sections of Units 2, 4, and 5.

Exercise Pages

Unit 1: Communication: Talking to Each Other

Chapter 3: Leave Me a Message

CATEGORIZING

1. Read the messages and decide what category each best belongs in. Write *W* for work, *S* for school, and *H* for home. Some messages might fit in more than one category.

SET B

a. _____ The paper is due next Thursday.

b. _____ We're out of milk. Pick up a few quarts.

c. _____ Judy wants you to meet her at the library to study for the final.

d. _____ Let's meet for lunch near my office and talk about the project.

2. Work with a partner to check your answers.

3. Work with a partner who chose the messages in Set A. Take turns reading to each other the messages in both Set A and Set B. Decide which categories your partner's messages belong in.

4. Now turn to page 25 and complete the activity.

Unit 5: Technology for Today's World
Chapter 13: Food for the Twenty-First Century

READING FROM THE NEWS: ASKING INFORMATION QUESTIONS

A. Student B: Work with the story that follows. (Student A works with the story on page 163.) Complete the following steps.

1. Read the information questions about your story.
2. Read the story to find the main idea.
3. Underline the important facts that give the answers to the questions.
4. Work with a partner who read the same story to compare the facts you underlined.
5. Take turns asking and answering each other's questions.
6. Write your answers in note form.
7. Use your notes and take turns explaining as much of the story as you can.

Information Questions

1. Who developed this technology?

2. What is it used for?

3. How does it work?

4. What are the benefits?

5. Where is it used?

■■

Story B: A Solar Cooker

The solar cooker is a great invention for sunny countries in which there are not many trees. It is a simple combination of aluminum foil inside a cardboard box that opens up to reflect the sun's rays and create heat. A dark-colored pot is placed inside the open box. The heat from the sun hits the foil and is transferred to the pot. The solar cooker can be used to boil water and to prepare food. This simple system was developed by workers of a company that advises rural citizens in African countries. The benefit to the people is that it saves the time it would take to find wood and the money that could be used to buy more food instead of wood or other kinds of fuel.

RETELLING THE STORY

1. Work with a partner who read story A. Explain your story to each other. Use the illustration to help you explain. Ask and answer each other's questions.

2. Together, make a list of the similarities and differences between your two stories. Share your ideas with your classmates.

3. Use the questions and answers to help you write about each of the stories.

Unit 6: Leisure

Chapter 16: Today's Workweek: Do We Need Time Out?

READING FROM THE NEWS: ASKING INFORMATION QUESTIONS

Student B: Work with the story that follows. (Student A works with the story on page 205.) Complete the following steps.

1. Read the information questions about your story.
2. Read to find out the main idea of the story.
3. Underline the important facts that give the answers to the questions.
4. Work with a partner who read the same story to compare the facts you underlined.
5. Take turns asking and answering each other's questions.
6. Write the answers in note form.
7. Use your notes and take turns explaining as much of the story as you can.

Information Questions

1. What kind of vacation is this?

2. What kind of people go on this type of vacation?

3. How expensive it is?

4. What are the attractions of this kind of vacation?

5. What are the disadvantages?

■ ■

Story B: Destination Solitude at the Nada Monastery

Many vacationers like to go to popular resorts where there are lots of people and activities. But not everyone likes this kind of vacation. The Nada Monastery is one example of the kind of vacation destination that is attracting people who are looking for some peace and quiet. The Nada Monastery is a retreat in the mountains of Colorado in the western United States. People who come to the monastery pay $300 (U.S.) a week for a cabin that is set back in the trees up in the hills. There people can eat simple vegetarian food and go for hikes on mountain trails or just sit and read or enjoy the view. The retreat is far from civilization; the closest town is 50 miles away. It's a good place to come, relax, and regain energy.

RETELLING THE STORY

1. **Work with a partner who read story A. Explain your story to each other. Ask and answer each other's questions.**

2. **Use the questions and answers to help you write about one of the stories.**

3. **Choose a similar short newspaper article from your local paper. Make a copy of the article and work with a partner. Follow the steps on page E-4 to prepare to discuss your article.**

Answer Key

UNIT 1 Communication: Talking to Each Other

CHAPTER 1 Reading Body Language

Getting Information from Illustrations, page 4

A. 1. 1 **2.** 5 **3.** 4 **4.** 3 **5.** 6 **6.** 2

Previewing the Titles, page 5

1. Eyes **3.** Hands **6.** Body **7.** Head

Understanding Details, pages 7–8

A. 1. b **2.** b **3.** a **4.** b **5.** a **6.** b **7.** a **8.** b
B. 1. "…you are staring." **2.** "…a handshake."
3. a. "OK" or "Very good" **b.** the opposite of what it is in North America **c.** an insult
d. money

Matching Ideas and Details, page 8

1. g **2.** d, e, f **3.** b **4.** a, c

Solving a Problem: Applying the Information, page 10

(sample answers)
1. Student Y may feel embarrassed to shake student X's hand, and student X may feel insulted that student Y is not taking his/her hand. Student X can explain that this is the way to say hello in his/her country, and student Y can show or explain how to say hello in his/her country.
2. The professor is angry because the student is late (tapping her pencil on the desktop) and may get angry with the student. The student can apologize to the professor for being late. **3.** The other friend may be embarrassed and uncomfortable at this kind of affection between a man and a woman. You can explain to this friend that this is a common way to greet a friend you haven't seen for a long time, according to your customs. **4.** You may feel confused or feel that the others may be talking about you. You can ask them what this hand signal means. **5.** She may be wondering why you are not looking at her instead of listening to what you are saying. You should look in her eyes sometimes or ask her whether she understands.

Vocabulary in Context, page 11

1. d **2.** a **3.** f **4.** c **5.** b **6.** e

Categorizing, page 11

1. people; because it is not a part of the body **2.** England; because it is not a continent
3. eyes; because it is the only body part **4.** thumb; because it is not an action **5.** OK; because it is not a greeting **6.** interested; because it is the only positive feeling

Personal Writing, page 12

(sample sentences) Body language can give you a lot of information. One day, I was talking to my friend, and she started stretching and looking around the room. She looked bored... .

CHAPTER 2 Communication Across Cultures

Understanding Details, pages 15–17

A. 1. the name of an apartment building **2.** in downtown Los Angeles **3.** because people who live there speak twelve different languages **4.** house of harmony and peace **5.** six languages
B. 1. a. different traditions and different customs **b.** try food from other cultures
2. special celebrations at the building **3.** Korea = *kimchi*; South America = dishes of roasted peppers **4.** a traditional turkey to every family **5.** cook the turkey in their own way
6. because people learn from one another how to enjoy new customs, such as traditional music and dances

Understanding Details, pages 18–20

A. 1. a. Spanish **b.** English **2.** a mixture of Spanish and English **3.** taking, for example, an English word and putting a Spanish-sounding ending on it **4.** taking an easy word in one language and using it in a sentence in another language **5. a.** It is easy and fun to speak.
b. It is easy and fun to understand (if you're bilingual).
B. 1. in New York, Miami, and Los Angeles **2.** on the community radio stations **3.** in popular magazines, novels, and poetry **4. a.** It sounds better. **b.** It helps express people's identity as both Spanish and American. **c.** It's creative and fits their lives today. **5.** joy, anger, and love

Comparing the Stories, pages 20–21

B. 1. F **2.** F **3.** F **4.** T **5.** F **6.** F
C. 3. People can learn new customs and languages, enjoy them, and make them their own.

Vocabulary in Context, pages 21–22

A. (sample answers)
1. a. People learn about different traditions and different customs from one another.
b. Trying food from other cultures is one of the exciting exchanges that people shared.
2. a. In New York City, two young Hispanic women are talking at lunch. **b.** Each woman speaks Spanish perfectly. **3. a.** People like to use Spanglish for various reasons. **b.** One man says it just sounds better.
B. 1. c **2.** b **3.** d **4.** e **5.** g **6.** a **7.** f

Categorizing, pages 22–23

1. Korea; Korean; *kumchi* **2.** South America; Spanish (Portuguese); roasted red peppers
3. Central America; Spanish; turkey in orange juice

Other answers will vary.

CHAPTER 3 Leave Me a Message

Categorizing, page 25

Set A: a. W   **b.** H   **c.** H   **d.** S

Exercise Pages, page 231

Set B: a. S   **b.** H   **c.** S   **d.** W
5. (sample messages)
   Friend: Meet me at the mall after class.
   Classmate: Sally needs your class notes for the exam.
   Family member: Your friend called while you were in the shower.
   Teacher: I left my paper with the secretary.

Matching, page 27

1. c   **2.** a   **3.** d   **4.** b

Understanding Details, pages 28–29

A. 1. c   **2.** a   **3.** a   **4.** a   **5.** b   **6.** c
B. 1. marriage proposal   **2.** her son's car   **3.** a scientist   **4.** a report, on the top
5. popular, the world

Applying the Information, pages 30–31

A. 1. b   **2.** d   **3.** a   **4.** e   **5.** c
B. 1. John   **2.** Nancy   **3.** Mona   **4.** Sam   **5.** John   **6.** Sam   **7.** Mona   **8.** Nancy
(sample messages)
John: Your boss called and said that you left your brushes at the client's house.
Nancy: The neighbor came by earlier to ask whether you would look at her cut.
Mona: The studio called to remind you of your ten o'clock session.
Sam: Don't forget to pay your fees today!

Vocabulary in Context, page 32

1. c   **2.** d   **3.** a   **4.** f   **5.** b   **6.** e

Prepositions, page 33

1. c   **2.** d   **3.** e   **4.** d   **5.** a   **6.** b, f

Verbs Present and Past, page 33

1. invented   **2.** needed   **3.** took   **4.** wrote   **5.** stuck   **6.** met

UNIT 2 The Mysteries of Sleep

CHAPTER 4 Sleep: How Much Is Not Enough?

Understanding Details, pages 43–44

A. 1. b **2.** a **3.** b **4.** a **5.** b **6.** a
B. 1. work, meetings, food **2.** gym, housework, cook **3.** chemicals, rest, healthy **4.** lose, body **5.** deep

Applying the Information: Problem Solving, pages 44–45

(sample answers)
1. Alice is too busy. She could stop studying until her children get a little older. **2.** Paul's schedule is too busy. He should cut down on something, such as his time online.

Vocabulary in Context, pages 45–46

A. 1. d **2.** a **3.** e **4.** f **5.** g **6.** b **7.** c
B. 1. V **2.** N **3.** V **4.** N **5.** N **6.** V
C. 1. c **2.** e **3.** b **4.** d **5.** a

CHAPTER 5 Sleep Problems

Understanding Details, pages 49–51

A. 1. 8 hours **2.** Great. He is rested and ready for the day. **3.** 3 hours **4.** snores
5. She moves to the couch to get some sleep. **6.** snoring
B. 1. tired and grumpy **2.** sleepy **3.** at a very long meeting at work **4.** She felt very hot and had a headache. **5.** She fell asleep. **6.** She is afraid of losing her job.
C. 1. a. Is he overweight? **b.** Does he smoke? **c.** Is he very tired? **2.** Yes, because they may be the cause of his snoring. **3.** a good strong mattress **4. a.** surgery **b.** a special breathing mask

Understanding Details, pages 53–55

A. 1. a. thirty-two years old. **b.** single. **c.** two: one fourteen and one nine years old
2. She has trouble falling asleep. **3.** the problems she has at work and about her children
4. because there are so many things to do for her children, and there is just not enough time for everything
B. 1. She gets up and does housework, or she works on the computer in her bedroom.
2. at 5:30 **3.** makes her kids their breakfast and their lunches and gets ready for work
4. 2 or 3 hours **5.** to stay awake **6.** Should she take drugs to fall asleep? What does she need to do?
C. 1. because of stress, pain, and other health problems **2.** take drugs **3.** work at night
4. make it quiet and comfortable **5.** write a list of the problems and some possible solutions
6. that she'll look at the list in the morning

Comparing the Stories, page 56

B. 1. F; Ann's problem is that her husband's snoring wakes her up; Judy's problem is that she can't fall asleep, because of too much stress.   **2.** F; Judy is single.   **3.** T   **4.** F; Only Judy is worried.   **5.** T   **6.** F; Ann gets advice about her husband's snoring problem; Judy gets advice about how to relax more.

Vocabulary in Context, page 58

1. a   **2.** e   **3.** d   **4.** b   **5.** g   **6.** c   **7.** f   **8.** i   **9.** h

Jigsaw Sentences, page 59

1. e   **2.** d   **3.** c   **4.** b   **5.** a

Categorizing, page 59

1. grumpy; because it is a mood, and the others are sleep states   **2.** mattress; because it is a piece of furniture, and the others are an amount of time   **3.** cool; because it is a temperature, and the others are all activities   **4.** coffee; because the others are a state of health

CHAPTER 6 Why Do We Dream?

Getting Information from Illustrations, page 63

1. five   **2.** the last one (fifth)

Understanding Details, pages 65–66

A. 1. T   **2.** F   **3.** F   **4.** F   **5.** T   **6.** T   **7.** F   **8.** T   **9.** T   **10.** T
B. 1. half of the time   **2.** as stories   **3.** dreams about feeling guilty for things that they did   **4.** work or their family   **5.** going to work on time or putting on clothes   **6.** their bus or plane or train, or they are late for an appointment   **7.** if you wake up during a dream   **8.** tell yourself your dream when you wake; keep a pen and paper or a tape recorder near your bed and write or record your dream   **9.** when they are worried

Evaluating the Information, page 67

1. b   **2.** e   **3.** d   **4.** c   **5.** a

Vocabulary in Context, page 68

1. c   **2.** j   **3.** f   **4.** l   **5.** d   **6.** b   **7.** a   **8.** e   **9.** k   **10.** i   **11.** g   **12.** h

Reading Cloze, page 71

1. k   **2.** a   **3.** c   **4.** h   **5.** g   **6.** a   **7.** b   **8.** d   **9.** j   **10.** i   **11.** k   **12.** e
13. f   **14.** b

UNIT 3 Relationships

CHAPTER 7 Is Dating Still the Same?
Understanding Details, pages 77–79

A. 1. T   **2.** T   **3.** F; in the past, men asked women out on dates   **4.** F; only Jerry does; Susan, only on special dates   **5.** T   **6.** T   **7.** T
B. 1. school dances, ballgames, church activities, and summer camp   **2.** at work or at the gym, through the Internet   **3.** only when she had a special date, such as a formal dance or the senior prom   **4.** Yes, he likes to wear things that make him look good.   **5.** It depends. If he asks someone out, he pays, but if she asks him out, he splits the bill.   **6.** In Susan's time, the cost of a date was about one day's pay, whereas the cost of Jerry's dates today are about half a week's pay.   **7.** sitting for hours and talking in a relaxed place, such as a coffee shop
C. 1. Susan   **2.** David   **3.** Susan   **4.** Susan   **5.** Jerry   **6.** Jerry   **7.** David   **8.** Jerry

Evaluating the Information: Categorizing, page 79

1. Susan: school dances, ballgames, church activities, and summer camp
   Jerry: work, gym, through an ad in the newspaper, bars or clubs, or through the Internet
2. Susan: usually, the man, unless they "go Dutch"
   Jerry: depends; if he asks someone out, he pays; if someone asks him out, they split the bill
3. Susan: about one day's pay
   Jerry: about half a week's pay
4. Susan: going to a little coffee shop and sitting for hours, talking
   Jerry: going somewhere that doesn't cost a lot of money, where you can relax and get to know each other, such as a bookstore café

Getting Information from Illustrations, page 80

1. 1970s   **2.** 1960s   **3.** 1980s   **4.** 1990s

Vocabulary in Context, page 81

1. f   **2.** g   **3.** b   **4.** c   **5.** a   **6.** d   **7.** e   **8.** h

Word Forms: Verbs, page 82

A. 1. did   **2.** met   **3.** dated   **4.** had   **5.** worked   **6.** paid   **7.** cost   **8.** was
B. (sample answers)
   Affirmative: **1.** The man waves goodbye to his daughter.   **2.** The man waved goodbye to his daughter.
   Negative: **1.** The man doesn't wave goodbye to his daughter.   **2.** The man didn't wave goodbye to his daughter.
   Questions: **1.** Is the man waving goodbye to his daughter?   **2.** Did the man wave goodbye to his daughter?

CHAPTER 8 A Different Kind of Wedding

Understanding Details, page 86

A. 1. a wedding gown, a choir to sing wedding songs, flowers, and a cake   **2.** It is not a legal wedding. She is planning to marry herself.   **3.** on June 27   **4.** because it is her fortieth birthday
B. 1. to celebrate and say that she is happy with her life   **2.** a ring   **3.** special songs, such as "My Way" by Frank Sinatra
C. 1. 200 friends and relatives   **2.** her fiancé   **3.** She may get legally married to her fiancé.
4. She is happy to be marrying herself.

Understanding Details, pages 90–92

A. 1. He is a graduate student in anthropology.   **2.** He is an independent and creative person.
3. He has a tuxedo, the rings, a minister, and musicians.   **4.** He is looking for a bride.
5. in the newspaper and on the Internet
B. 1. to a special reception before the wedding ceremony   **2.** their friends and families
3. They will interview the brides-to-be.   **4.** They will interview Dave.   **5.** the winner
C. 1. He really wants to get married.   **2.** "the right woman"   **3.** He is not happy; he thinks that his son should take marriage more seriously.   **4.** a marriage counselor   **5.** He doesn't think that Dave's plan will work.   **6.** He doesn't think that friends can choose a good partner for you; only you can choose that person.

Vocabulary in Context, pages 95–96

1. c   **2.** d   **3.** e   **4.** b   **5.** f   **6.** a   **7.** g

Matching Meanings, page 96

1. e   **2.** c   **3.** g   **4.** f   **5.** h   **6.** a   **7.** b   **8.** d
(sample sentence) **1.** My *wife* wanted a *traditional* wedding.

Categorizing, page 97

1. strength, because it is not a part of a marriage   **2.** counselor, because it is a person, not an adjective   **3.** unusual, because it is not a type of relationship   **4.** sing, because it is an external, not internal, process/activity   **5.** apartment, because it is not part of a wedding ceremony

CHAPTER 9 Neighbors

Matching Meanings, page 99

A. 1. b   **2.** a

Note Taking: Finding the Key Words, pages 102–103

A.

Cynthia	Ann
1. a. Single	Single
b. Works in an office	A lawyer
c. Yes, four	Yes, two

2. **a.** It is difficult for her to work all day
     and put dinner on the table every night
     for her kids.

Hard having to cook and clean after working
all day

   b. Tired

Impatient and angry

   c. To spend her food budget on expensive
       take-out food

To be angry

   d. To give her kids a well-balanced
       nutritious meal

To spend more time with her kids at home

   e. To take turns cooking for each other's
       families once a week

To take turns cooking for each other's families
once a week

3. PEOPLE AND PROBLEMS

HELP THAT SOME PEOPLE CAN OFFER

   a. Older people who can no longer drive or
       take public transportation to do their
       grocery shopping on their own

Groups that take these older people so they
can do their grocery shopping

   b. People's homes that may be robbed or
       other crimes

Neighborhood crime-watch groups that keep
an eye on people's homes and watch for any
signs of crime

   c. Children who may need a safe home in
       case of emergency

Child-safety programs that ask adults to watch
out for neighborhood children

4. **a.** They talk about their problems and responsibilities.

b. They discuss the neighborhood school their young children attend.

B. **1.** T   **2.** F   **3.** F   **4.** F   **5.** T   **6.** F   **7.** T   **8.** F   **9.** F   **10.** T

Vocabulary in Context, pages 104–105

A. **1.** d   **2.** e   **3.** b   **4.** f   **5.** g   **6.** c

B. **1.** N (sample sentence) She needs a lot of attention.

2. N (sample sentence) She works very hard.

3. V (sample sentence) The help people get from these charities is great.

4. V (sample sentence) She gave me her share of the pie.

5. V (sample sentence) The budget for this year is $100.

6. N (sample sentence) I drive every day to work.

7. V (sample sentence) The sign on the road said "STOP."

Prepositions, page 106

1. b, d   **2.** a, b   **3.** d, b   **4.** d, b   **5.** e   **6.** f

Reading Cloze, page 108

1. j   **2.** a   **3.** h   **4.** i   **5.** a   **6.** e   **7.** k   **8.** b   **9.** b   **10.** c   **11.** f   **12.** d   **13.** g

UNIT 4 The Challenge of Sports Today

CHAPTER 10 The Challenge of the Triathlon

Getting Information from Illustrations, page 113

A. 1. c   **2.** a   **3.** d   **4.** b

Understanding the Main Ideas, page 116

1. C   **2.** B   **3.** A

Understanding Details, pages 116–117

A. 1. c   **2.** b   **3.** a   **4.** b   **5.** c   **6.** c
B. 1. It takes a lot of strength and willpower to compete.   **2.** Because they wanted to make their training exciting.   **3.** In 1982, it became famous because of the televised performance of Julie Moss.   **4.** Three meters before the line, she fell down. She tried to get up, but she kept falling. She finally crawled across the finish line.   **5.** Special people who have time in their lives for careers and family. Many triathletes are happily married.

Antonyms, page 119

1. g   **2.** b   **3.** c   **4.** f   **5.** e   **6.** a   **7.** d

(sample sentence) **1.** He said goodbye to the *single* life when he got *married*.

Word Form, pages 119–120

1. bicycling   **2.** training   **3.** race   **4.** swimming   **5.** run

Vocabulary in Context, page 120

A. 1. d   **2.** g   **3.** h   **4.** e   **5.** c   **6.** f   **7.** b, a

CHAPTER 11 Looking for Excitement

Understanding the Main Ideas, page 124

1. B   **2.** A   **3.** C

Understanding Details, pages 124–127

A. 1. They head for the mountains.   **2.** It is fun and exciting. It's like surfing on the snow.
3. Wide, like surfboards, and there are places on the boards to strap them to your feet.
4. They move back and forth in wide curves.   **5.** They like to jump and turn as they speed down the mountains.
B. 1. young people in their teens and twenties   **2.** Because it was fast and challenging. They could do special tricks on the board, such as turning over or jumping over bumps in the snow.
3. wore special clothes and used a special vocabulary to talk about their moves   **4.** They did not like them, because of their fast and unusual movements. Sometimes, snowboarders damaged the ski paths and made it dangerous for the skiers coming down the mountain.   **5.** Some ski resorts banned snowboarders and didn't allow them on the hills, because of the skiers' complaints.

C. 1. Fifty percent of the people who visit ski resorts will be snowboarders.   **2.** internationally, because it has become an Olympic sport   **3.** people of all ages   **4.** 40   **5. a.** They welcome snowboarders to share the hills with skiers.   **b.** The number of people trying the sport is up 200 percent.

Understanding the Main Ideas, page 130

1. C   **2.** B   **3.** A

Understanding Details, page 130–132

A. 1. climbing boots and other climbing equipment   **2. a.** in parks or other places   **b.** city gyms, on special climbing walls   **3.** It goes straight up and has small holding places for hands and feet.
B. 1. special shoes and a harness around your chest to hold you   **2.** The ropes attach to your harness. They hold you in place so that you don't fall.   **3.** There are small pieces of metal that stick out for you to stand on and hold on to.   **4.** to control your fear   **5.** The harness and ropes hold you, and you begin to feel safe.   **6.** At the top, the teacher slowly releases the rope, and then you slide back to the floor. Your arms and legs feel tired, but you feel great.
C. 1. It is good exercise.   **2.** almost anyone   **3.** You use your whole body, especially your arms and legs.   **4.** It gives your body a complete workout. You strengthen your mind as well as your body.

Vocabulary in Context, page 135

A. 1. fast   **2.** hardest   **3.** special climbing   **4.** average   **5.** popular   **6.** complete
7. wide
B. 1. d   **2.** c   **3.** b   **4.** a

CHAPTER 12 Training for the Olympics Today: What Does It Take?

Getting Information from a Chart, pages 138–139

A. 1. in 1896, 300 athletes; in 1996, 10,000 athletes   **2.** Now, 190 countries come, 175 more than in 1896.   **3.** In 1896, only amateurs were allowed, but in 1996, amateurs and professional were allowed.   **4.** very little in 1896; on live television around the world in 1996

Understanding the Main Idea, page 141

1. C   **2.** A   **3.** B

Identifying Supporting Points and Details, page 142

1. S   **2.** D   **3.** D   **4.** S   **5.** S   **6.** D

Vocabulary in Context, pages 145–146

A. 1. a. train   **b.** trained   **2.** produces   **3.** went   **4.** takes   **5.** teach, taught
B. 1. g   **2.** a   **3.** b   **4.** f   **5.** d   **6.** c   **7.** e   **8.** h

Reading Cloze, page 149

1. f   **2.** e   **3.** g   **4.** b   **5.** h   **6.** c   **7.** c   **8.** a   **9.** j   **10.** h   **11.** i   **12.** d

UNIT 5 Technology for Today's World

CHAPTER 13 Food for the Twenty-First Century

Understanding Details, pages 156–158

A. 1. a   **2.** b   **3.** a   **4.** c   **5.** a   **6.** a

B. 1. because scientists think that in 20 or 30 years, astronauts will be living in space colonies, and this would be an inexpensive way to be able to feed these people   **2. a.** special mixtures of chemicals   **b.** artificial lights   **c.** climate-controlled rooms   **3.** They can grow vegetables, such as lettuce, tomatoes, and cucumbers and many different herbs and spices.

4. Hydroponic Vegetables Now   Hydroponic Vegetables for Space Colonies

a. Lettuce	Rice
b. Tomatoes	Beans
c. Cucumbers	Potatoes
d. Herbs and spices	Wheat

5. They are experimenting with recipes that use hydroponic vegetables. They make imitation meat dishes, such as carrot drumsticks, made from carrots, peppers, onions, garlic, herbs, and breadcrumbs, instead of chicken.   **6. a.** 25 taste testers   **b.** They taste five different dishes.   **c.** They decide what tastes good or not.

Applying the Information: Making an Argument, pages 159–160

1. How practical and necessary it is for Cornell to experiment on making food that can be grown out in space.   **2.** (sample answer) With pollution increasing on Earth every day, this may be another way to make sure that we have access to safer foods in the future.   **3.** (sample answer) There is too much money already being spent on the space program.

Vocabulary in Context, pages 160–161

A. 1. b   **2.** e   **3.** c   **4.** b   **5.** a
B. 1. artificial lights   **2.** soil   **3.** natural climate   **4.** tofu, seitan
C. 1. artificial lights   **2.** They use tofu and seitan.

Reading from the News: Asking Information Questions, page 162

Story A: Wheeling Water

1. South African architect Hans Hendrikse and his brother Piet, a civil engineer   **2.** to carry water   **3.** It is a round, thick drum with a hole in the middle. You fill the drum with water, screw on the lid, and roll the drum along the ground.   **4.** You can pull the drum with a rope that goes through the middle. It is easier to carry water than by the old method of carrying it in buckets or in jars on backs.   **5.** in Kenya, Ethiopia, Tanzania, Namibia, and South Africa

Story B: A Solar Cooker, Exercise Pages, page E–3

1. workers of a company that advises rural citizens in African countries   **2.** It is used to boil water and to prepare food.   **3.** It is a simple combination of aluminum foil inside a simple cardboard box that opens up to reflect the sun's rays and to create heat. A dark-colored pot is placed inside the open box. The heat from the sun hits the foil and is transferred to the pot.   **4.** It saves the time it would take to find wood and the money that could be used to buy more food instead of wood or other kinds of fuel.   **5.** in sunny countries in which there are not many trees; in African countries

CHAPTER 14 New Ways to Keep in Touch

Understanding the Main Ideas, page 166

A. There are many advantages of having a cell phone.
B. There are many disadvantages of having a cell phone.

Understanding Details, pages 166–168

A. 1. It is very easy because you can call people and receive calls anytime and anywhere.
2. Analog and digital phones: they use both radio waves and telephone lines.   **3. a.** to be able to receive a call while you are already talking   **b.** It shows you the name of the caller on your cell phone.   **4. a.** send and receive faxes   **b.** make notes to yourself on the phone
5. a. They are getting smaller and cheaper.   **b.** You can use them to reach people anywhere in the world.   **c.** They are good in an emergency if you need to call for help.
B. 1. when the battery is low   **2.** They lost their phone service when a communications satellite failed.   **3.** because more and more car accidents happen while people are talking on their cell phones   **4.** when they are at the movies or in a class at school   **5.** when they are traveling on the bus or standing in line at the supermarket

Recapping the Story: Highlighting, page 169

1. use radio waves and telephone lines   **2.** anywhere   **3.** make and receive calls, send and receive faxes, make notes to yourself on the phone   **4.** Cell phones are getting smaller and cheaper. They are convenient because you can call anytime from any location. You can reach people anywhere in the world. They are good in an emergency if you need to call for help.
5. Cell phones don't operate well when the battery is low. You can lose phone service when a communication satellite fails. They can be dangerous to use when you drive. Conversations are not private, because people can listen in by picking up the same radio frequency used for the calls. Other people don't like to hear them ringing at the movies or in class or hearing people's private conversations while in a bus or in line at the supermarket. Some cell phone companies charge quite a bit of money for using the service during certain times. They can be expensive and annoying.

Understanding the Main Ideas, page 171

A. There are many uses and advantages to having e-mail.
B. There are disadvantages of having e-mail.

Understanding Details, pages 171–173

A. 1. write, send, and receive messages   **2.** because you don't have to pay for long-distance calls   **3.** anyone else who has an e-mail account   **4.** to 50 people or more   **5. a.** People in offices can communicate with one another.   **b.** You can work without having to go into the office, by dialing up your office computer and transferring the files you need to your home computer.   **6.** They are becoming as common as phone numbers.
B. 1. annoying junk mail and messages they aren't interested in   **2.** It takes time to check and clear your e-mail box; sometimes, the lines are busy, and it's difficult to get online and log on; sometimes, the system crashes and can't be used.   **3.** They feel that receiving handwritten letters and cards in the mail is more satisfying.   **4. a.** They can send e-mail to the wrong person.
b. An office worker complained about his boss in an e-mail to another employee, but then he pressed the wrong key to send it, and everyone in the office got the mail, including his boss.

Recapping the Story, page 174

1. You connect your computer and modem to a phone line; with a service provider, you can have an e-mail account.   **2.** It can be used all over the world to send and receive messages.
3. You can send an instant message to anyone else who has an e-mail account; you can send the same message to 50 people or more.   **4.** no long distance charges; can use it to communicate with people all around the world; can use it to communicate with people during work or even work from home by transferring files from work to your home computer   **5.** receive annoying junk mail; it can take time to check and clear your e-mail box; waste time when lines are busy and it's difficult to log on or the system crashes; can make a mistake and send e-mail to the wrong person

Vocabulary in Context, pages 175–176

A. 1. "e" for electronic   **2.** short for cellular   **3.** short for facsimiles, such as documents and other printed material   **4.** shows you the name of the caller   **5.** to receive a call while you are already talking
B. 1. d   **2.** e   **3.** b   **4.** f   **5.** g   **6.** c   **7.** j   **8.** i   **9.** a   **10.** h

Topic Writing—Comparing Technologies, page 178

(sample sentences) E-mail (e for electronic) is a great invention. You can send and receive messages anywhere and at any time of the day. Another advantage is… .

CHAPTER 15 The Internet Offers an Eye on the World

Understanding Details, page 183

1. She starts work at 9 and finishes at 6. She works all week and sometimes has to travel.
2. He is at the day-care center from 8:30 until 6:30.   **3.** Whenever she wants. The day-care center has a video camera that is connected to a special, secure Web site. When she wants to see him, she can call up the Web site on her computer and see the center on her screen.
4. Wonderful. One time, she dropped Harry off at the center, and he started to cry. She had to leave, but he wouldn't stop crying. She was so worried at work, she couldn't concentrate, so she went to the Web site and saw that Harry was playing a game and looked happy. She felt a lot better.   **5.** At first, they felt self-conscious, but now they don't seem to notice, and activities go on as usual.   **6.** It depends. Usually, about four or five times a day.   **7.** She likes what she sees. There is a variety of interesting activities; the children get individual attention; she recommended the center to two friends.

Understanding Examples, page 184

1. 1st: He started to cry.
   2nd: She couldn't concentrate at work.
   3rd: She logged on to see that Harry was happy.
   Feeling: better—a relief
2. 1st: Harry wrote "Hi, Grandpa."
   2nd: Father was happy.
   3rd: wrote an e-mail right away
   Feeling: It's like we're living in the same house.

Applying the Information: Problem Solving, page 185

(sample notes) *Benefit:* People who live far away can take the course without leaving their houses. *Question:* How could you prevent cheating?

Vocabulary in Context, pages 186–187

A. 1. b **2.** e **3.** g **4.** d **5.** h **6.** a **7.** f **8.** c
B. 1. d **2.** e **3.** c **4.** a **5.** b

Topic Writing, page 189

(sample notes) One advantage of the Internet is that you can log on anytime of day. One disadvantage is that the system can crash.

Reading Cloze, page 190

1. b **2.** a **3.** d **4.** f **5.** h **6.** c **7.** i **8.** e **9.** j **10.** g

UNIT 6 Leisure

CHAPTER 16 Today's Workweek: Do We Need Time Out?

Understanding Details, pages 198–200

A. 1. the same hours **2.** decrease to 30 hours or less **3.** "When will I get some free time?"
4. People have to work longer hours or work at a second job. **5.** do more work with fewer workers **6.** taking their work home with them on the weekends and in the evenings **7.** They checked their voice mail or answering machine once during their vacation. Some people even checked their voice or e-mail once a day.
B. 1. a. The increase in the cost of living. People work longer hours or have a second job to be able to support a family today. **b.** Many companies are trying to do more work with fewer workers, so employees are often asked and feel as though they have no choice but to work overtime. **2.** Because it costs so much to support her family and that working less is not possible. This situation is related to the increase in the cost of living. **3.** Because her boss wants the job done. If she doesn't finish the work at home, in 16 hours, he thinks that she is not really working at home. This situation is related more to the second reason: employees feel that they have no choice but to work overtime. **4. a.** on the weekends, in the evenings when they are home with their families **b.** on vacation **5.** Because if she doesn't finish her work in 16 hours, her boss thinks that she is not really working at home. **6. a.** We may never get to leave the office, at least not for long. **b.** People may begin to say, "This is enough; I need my leisure time."

Understanding Examples, page 200

	LILY	ELAINE
Profile:	Works in New Jersey; single mother with two children	Mother of nine-month-old baby
Work they do:	A social worker; sees private clients at home office; caterer	Works for an insurance company

Personal Background:	Single mother with two children	Mother of nine-month-old baby; works a flexible shedule
Reasons for working long hours:	It costs so much to support her family.	Her boss doesn't believe that she works at home if she doesn't complete the work.

Vocabulary in Context, pages 202–203

A. 1. a **2.** c **3.** d **4.** g **5.** b **6.** f **7.** e
B. 1. d **2.** c **3.** a **4.** e **5.** g **6.** b **7.** f

Antonyms, page 203

1. d **2.** h **3.** b **4.** i **5.** e **6.** c **7.** a **8.** j **9.** f **10.** g

Reading from the News: Asking Information Questions, page 204

Story A: Taking a Trip in the Car
1. a car trip/vacation **2.** American, mostly with middle-class background; a majority with a university education **3.** It is not very expensive, because they save money by taking the car. **4.** saving money and the sense of control and freedom they get being behind the wheel **5.** the possibility of car trouble on the road

Story B: Destination Solitude at the Nada Monastery, Exercise Pages, page E–4
1. the Nada Monastery, a retreat in the mountains of Colorado **2.** people who are looking for some peace and quiet **3.** $300 (U.S.) a week for a cabin that is set back in the trees up in the hills **4.** good place to go, relax, and regain their energy **5.** It is far from civilization.

CHAPTER 17 Entertainment Choices

Categorizing, page 206

1. V **2.** B **3.** M **4.** V **5.** V

Listing Advantages, page 207

(sample reason) **1.** It's relaxing.

Understanding the Main Ideas, page 207

A. There are positive things about watching TV during the week.
B. There are advantages of watching movies at home on the weekend.

Understanding Details, pages 207–210

A. 1. to stay at home, eat, and watch TV **2.** all night, 24 hours a day **3.** two **4.** 24 hours a day **5. a.** documentaries **b.** sit-coms **c.** dramatic shows **6.** no; well, not exactly
B. 1. goes to the video store and gets a few good movies and watches them on the VCR
2. It costs less, and you can really get comfortable. Also, you can pause the video and get up to get something to eat. **3.** Because his/her television is not in the living room, where the couch is. **4.** in the bedroom **5. a.** insomnia **b.** watching so much TV

Listing Advantages, page 212

(sample reason) **1.** It's fun to be with a lot of people.

Understanding the Main Ideas, page 212

A. the positive things about going out to see movies on a big screen
B. the social aspect of going to see movies

Understanding Details, pages 212–214

A. 1. go out to the movies   **2.** because of the equipment and the acoustics in the theater
3. The special effects don't look or sound as good at home.   **4.** The reaction of the crowd can intensify his/her feelings.   **5.** They can be really funny, and they help him/her decide what film to see when it comes out.
B. 1. enjoys going out to see movies and making an evening out of it   **2.** go have coffee with a friend   **3.** might go back two or three times, if the film is very moving or extremely well done
4. ticket price is lower   **5.** old classics or movies by a well-known director

Matching Meanings, page 216

1. d   **2.** h   **3.** f   **4.** i   **5.** c   **6.** a   **7.** e   **8.** g   **9.** b

(sample sentence) They overlooked her for the promotion again, because she was not appreciated.

Categorizing, page 216

1. station; because it is not about time   **2.** channels; because it is not a type of show
3. previews; because it is not a part of the movie you are watching   **4.** video store; because it is not a part of a home   **5.** interesting; because it's the only descriptive word

CHAPTER 18 Meeting at the Mall: America's Growing Leisure Activity

Matching, page 219

1. c   **2.** f   **3.** a   **4.** h   **5.** b   **6.** d   **7.** e   **8.** g

Previewing, page 219

1. B   **2.** C   **3.** A   **4.** D

Understanding Details, page 222

1. the mall   **2. a.** more than 300 malls   **b.** more than 200 different shops
3. a. Bloomington, Minnesota   **b.** more than 400 stores   **c.** 50 restaurants   **d.** 9 nightclubs
e. in 1995, about 40 million people   **4. a.** People visiting from overseas want to buy presents to bring home to families and friends.   **b.** Some tourists want to experience "consumer heaven."   **5. a.** "Now that we've seen the tourist sights, we can go home."   **b.** Some people plan their vacations around their shopping plans.   **c.** "consumer heaven"   **6. a.** teens
b. seniors

Listing Facts, page 223

1.

	GROUP A	GROUP B
Activity:	Daily hike	Socializing/talking
When:	At 7:00 A.M.	After school/on weekends
How long:	Until after breakfast	Most of the afternoon
Advantages:	It's a safe place, protected from the weather, quiet at 7:00 A.M. (avoid crowds)	Can socialize and talk, without spending too much money

2. a. *Positive effects:* They provide jobs and taxes for the government.   *Negative effects:* traffic jams, crowds, and low-paying jobs for most people who work there

Who Said That, page 223

1. T   **2.** TE   **3.** TE   **4.** S   **5.** TE   **6.** T   **7.** TE

Evaluating the Information: Reading from the News, page 224

1. holding services in retail malls as an added attraction to one-stop Sunday shopping   **2.** to bring new members to churches that are in financial trouble   **3.** out in the marketplace **4.** It has been a mixed success. They are attracting a lot of people. There's a lot of energy, but it doesn't feel like a church to some people.

Vocabulary in Context, page 225

1. e   **2.** g   **3.** h   **4.** j   **5.** f   **6.** a   **7.** d   **8.** c   **9.** b   **10.** i

Word Form, page 226

1. V   **2.** N   **3.** N   **4.** N   **5.** N   **6.** N   **7.** V

(sample sentence) Exercise is good for you.

Reading Cloze, page 229

1. j   **2.** i   **3.** e   **4.** f   **5.** c   **6.** b   **7.** a   **8.** h   **9.** g   **10.** d